ONE WAY

OTHER WORKS BY BERNARD BINLIN DADIÉ

NOVEL

Climbié (Paris: Éditions Seghers, 1956)

TRAVEL

Un Nègre à Paris (Paris: Présence Africaine, 1959)

La Ville où nul ne meurt (Paris: Présence Africaine, 1968)

POETRY

Afrique debout! (Paris: Éditions Seghers, 1950)

La Ronde des jours (Paris: Présence Africaine, 1956)

SHORT STORIES

Commandant Taureault et ses Nègres (Abidjan: Ceda-Hatier, 1980)

Les Jambes du fils de Dieu (Paris: Ceda-Hatier, 1980)

TALES AND POEMS

Hommes de tous les continents (Paris: Présence Africaine, 1967)

TALES

Légendes africaines (Paris: Éditions Seghers, 1954)

Le Pagne noir (Paris: Présence Africaine, 1955)

Contes de Koutou-as-Samala (Paris: Présence Africaine, 1982)

PLAYS

Monsieur Thôgô-gnini (Paris: Présence Africaine, 1970)

Béatrice au Congo (Paris: Présence Africaine, 1971)

Sidi: Maître Escroc; Situation difficile; Serment d'amour (Paris: Présence Africaine, 1971)

Ils de tempête (Paris: Présence Africaine, 1973)

Mhoi-Ceul (Paris: Présence Africaine, 1979)

ONE WAY
BERNARD DADIÉ OBSERVES AMERICA

BERNARD BINLIN DADIÉ

Translated by Jo Patterson

Foreword by Claude Bouygues

University of Illinois Press

URBANA AND CHICAGO

Published by agreement with the Société Nouvelle Présence Africaine
Manufactured in the United States of America
1 2 3 4 5 C P 5 4 3 2 1

This book is printed on acid-free paper.

Library of Congress Cataloging-in-Publication Data

Dadié, Bernard Binlin, 1916–
[Patron de New York. English]
One way : Bernard Dadié observes America / Bernard Binlin Dadié : translated by Jo Patterson ; foreword by Claude Bouygues.
p. cm.
Translation of: Un patron de New York.
ISBN 0-252-02039-1 (alk. paper).—ISBN 0-252-06408-9 (pbk: alk. paper)
1. United States—Civilization—1945– 2. Afro-Americans. 3. Africans—Travel—United States. 4. Dadié, Bernard Binlin, 1916– —Journeys—United States. I. Title.
E169.12.D3213 1994
973'.0496073—dc20 93-27875
CIP

FOREWORD
DADIÉ TRANS-VISITED

I COULD NOT be indifferent to anything about Dadié, including this translation of *Patron de New York,* since that day in 1957 when *Climbié,* recently published in Paris, fell into my hands in a small town in southern Tunisia. To put it "à la Giono," that is to say, alliteratively, I read *Climbié* in the midst of clamoring young Tunisian schoolchildren whom the French Republic entrusted to its teachers in the Franco-Arab schools of the Maghreb.

As I stood in the middle of that African playground, I realized that Dadié's work revealed a truth about myself and about Africa. That's a lot to claim for one book—it makes it unforgettable. For example, I immediately recognized the famous "symbol" at the beginning: it was the same terrible instrument of humiliation and petty betrayals that, as a child from the Occitan part of France, I had to carry during class or breaks at my small vilage school, but at arm's length and in the guise of a *Petit Larousse,* because I had spoken in the dialect, the language of local games and lullabies. (Will we ever really know how many scores get settled in secret on the so-called school playgrounds all over the world?) And here an African was teaching me the alienating power and repressive force of this symbol, and was warning me through his novel never to use it.

As for the tam-tam at the end of the novel, what a powerful symbol of Otherness and what a message for the naive colonizer! "How can I rule this continent, these people, when, every night, the drums hold them to the past?"[1] But I have often wondered why Dadié gave the last word in *Climbié* to Monsieur Tage, a European—Ouloguem would have had little use for him.

With Dadié, even at the heart of an anecdote or in the midst of a story we are never very far from the acid sting, the weighty purpose behind the discourse, or the moral lesson. This was true for *Climbié;* it is even truer for *Patron de New York,* now available in this translation by Jo Patterson.

1. From Karen Chapman's translation of *Climbié* (London: Heinemann Educational Books, 1971).

*
* *

It is fortunate that *Patron de New York,* along with *Un Nègre à Paris* (*An African in Paris*) and *La Ville où nul ne meurt* (*The City Where No One Dies*) is finally available to English-speaking readers with the especially appropriate title *One Way,* as it might reactivate studies and research on Dadié. In fact, this great writer has been unjustly neglected by contemporary theory and criticism in vogue in African or Afro-American studies, which are almost exclusively preoccupied with questions of formal and/or narratological divergences or philosophical speculations (for example, Mudimbé, Houtondji).

With *Patron de New York,* the itinerary is complete. Paris, Rome, New York, these are the capitals of Dadié's distress or, rather, the stages in his travels through the land of Anti-Africa. For at no time, in *Patron* or in the two prior wings of the triptych, does Dadié abandon, under the guise of a French stylist, either his African nature or his African vision. The style is so stilted, sometimes so tight-fitting, that it almost makes one uncomfortable. This poses certain problems and offers certain advantages, a few of which I would like to mention briefly.

First, some problems or concerns. The penetrating force of Dadié's Africanness, apparently an irrepressible biological trait, is so great that it makes him, perhaps more obviously than anywhere else, irreparably impervious to the Other. Thus, the documentary value of his observations on America is warped by the way he systematically superimposes upon the U.S. a grid which is the result of diametrically opposed cultural values. In this, he is doing nothing more than Céline did in *Le Voyage,* but he is somewhat more amused by, and detached from, the personal drama, and absolutely convinced that he can escape the disaster by returning to the refuge of his own country.

Dadié is, after a fashion, an African Mark Twain practicing his surgery on America; but at times—in his fulminations against New York City and in his evocations of Harlem, for example, and elsewhere in his poetry (see in particular "Harlem" and "Jour sur Harlem" in *Hommes de tous les Continents* [Paris: Présence Africaine, 1967])—he doubles as a Senghor (clearly echoing the famous poem "New York") who would have read *Banjo* and would try, ahead of his time, to improvise on the theme of the "Signifying Monkey."

There are more problems, some of which are rather serious ones. For instance, how can anyone even tour, much less understand, America without knowing English? Dadié, as he freely admits, has at his disposal a two-entry code system, Yes/No, in order to communicate linguistically with the Other, and so backs himself into a corner of caricature or incomprehension. This explains the almost total absence of dialogue. But it must be noted that the rare exchanges between Dadié and the Americans he meets are very funny, albeit facile. Nevertheless, Dadié knows enough English to indulge occasionally in some lighthearted wordplay. For example, he plays on the terms *bond* 'to jump' in French and *bond* 'marriage' in English (is he suggesting marriage is a leap?)

Dadié may not know English, but he is a cosmopolitan man. He is not a displaced or uprooted person, deprived of language or culture. He does not travel to America to forget his past or to build a future for himself: he arrives there already full of his personal dreams. He does not allow himself to be mesmerized by the impressive American machine. He passes through and observes (note Patterson's judicious choice of subtitle, *Bernard Dadié Observes America*). In his journey, he looks down on both people and things with extreme indignation and yet with unfailing good humor.

The keenness of Dadié's observations strikes the reader. He pitilessly exposes all the idiosyncracies of the American people and their lifestyle, from the most benign to the most disturbing, handling them all with the candor basic to his personality—mood swings included—using the widest range of tones, from humor to cynicism, including irony, sarcasm, and even admonishment. Thus, he reprimands the Americans for their obsession with abbreviations and acronyms (for example, "X-mas"), suggesting, as the root of the obsession, the will to compress both time and space which is, all things considered, typical of industrialized societies. He describes American superstition with irony; he is astounded by dating, by funerals, by cars, by the importance of sugar; he indulges in oversimplified caricatures, for example, to describe the origins of the Civil War and the Boston Tea Party.

Beneath the obviously biased perspective, Dadié's vision is surprisingly accurate; by some power of divination, this vision lends the text some strangely contemporary accents. For example: "A smoked peace is ready to be canned and the United States of America is preparing, tomorrow, to send tons of peace to the entire world" (p. 73). This is the post-Communist New World Order ahead of its time, no less. Dadié had seen it clearly, even if his thought is wrapped in floating anxiety.

While the message is extremely forceful from the very beginning and seems to remain so throughout the text, sometimes to the saturation point, there are, fortunately, many compensations: on the one hand, the use of humor and its avatars as mentioned above and, on the other, the sincerity of the feelings and ideas.

In fact this book contains breathtaking passages where the unadulterated voice of the African comes through, rightly surprised and shocked by the incessant activity, the sprawling life, the agitation in every direction, all of which strike him from the moment of his first contact with the U.S. and stay with him throughout. It seems that the best moments of righteous indignation are concentrated at the end of the text, delivered sometimes in powerful periodic sentences. Thus, the following passage where Dadié almost gets carried away speaking against the lack of restful nights in America: "Indeed America needs nighttime," lamenting that, as if by a sort of madness, the natural and vital rhythmical division between destructive day and healing night has been shattered. This is, in some way, a prose version of Senghor's poem "New York."

As for the structure, under the deluge of jumbled attacks, barbs, and witticisms throughout the entire text, the steady deep bass note of several thematic tam-tam beats can be heard. One lexical and semantic theme dominates the entire book and unifies it: liberty. It is often conveyed by the famous Statue of Liberty and serves as thematic and subthematic anchoring throughout the book. Among other major themes, it is obviously necessary to mention the "*One Way*" leitmotif, which appears in English in Dadié's original and the central importance of which the translator has recognized in the title of the English version.

Among the numerous benefits of reactivating this text with a good English translation is one of a not just literary but also a critical nature, leading up to social and personal analysis—thus connecting with one of Dadié's fundamental preoccupations: an interest in what is human. I think it is rewarding to go beyond the irritation which can be caused by the distorted images sometimes reflected by the mirror of the Other. In some way, American readers, especially American students, are invited to deconstruct: here they have a text where their country is seen from the place where one judges *Otherly*.

*

* *

The qualities of Jo Patterson's translation speak for themselves, in language the accuracy of which matches Dadié's. It was not an easy task because the prose in *Patron de New York* reveals Dadié's perfect mastery of the various stylistic devices in French, from synecdoche to paradox ("Les peuples de couleur ne sont sans doute pas les Nègres, ni les Jaunes ou les Rouges, mais certainement les Blancs"), including such classical Latin structures as the ablative absolute ("depuis John Brown pendu"), all used to communicate strong and complex ideas. Let us note in passing that contemporary critics (H. L. Gates among others) denounce this mastery of the language of the Other as indicating failure, a surrender to the criterion of perfectibility which is, in fact, one of the signs of imperialism, the imperial "odeur du père."

Patterson has succeeded in translating Dadié in language that is appropriate for the register of *Patron de New York* and, as is the case with good translations, she achieves a clarity which easily resolves ambiguities, non sequiturs, and other difficulties in the original text. In this regard, we can be glad that the translator has not hesitated to resort to Dadié's opinion in borderline cases. For, as is well known, if the author does not know everything about his book, he still remains the most reliable reader of it. If there are divergences, as in every translation of a work like *Patron de New York,* they will be found to be justified in order to clarify the original text.

Let me quote at random several successful passages which show the skill of the translator in those risky moments in translation such as, among others, modulations, reductions, and amplifications; in other words, the moments when the translator has freedom of choice.

As an example of a sound choice in shortening the French text, at the same time a little too unnecessarily heavy and marked with orality, "Mais l'Américain est-il véritablement un Cyclope? La question posée, mérite d'être débattue" becomes in Patterson's translation "The question 'Is the American really a Cyclops?' is debatable" (130/69). Elsewhere (129/69) in "maisons enrochées" the neologism is skillfully dodged and the substantive changed to "buildings," which is logically called for by the context. Later (226/120) "école du mensonge" is translated by a deft use of modulation as "Con U.," which conforms perfectly to the context of the dialogue in progress. In short, examples abound where the translator, aided by a very sure intuition, found the felicitous turn of phrase.

The translation *One Way* is timely, completing Dadié's trilogy in English. There is no doubt that its appearance will contribute greatly to making its author better known to Anglophone readers, and, we hope, will inspire new research and work on Dadié.

TRANSLATOR'S NOTE

I HAVE NOT changed Dadié's exclusive language, but such terms as *man* and *men* do not in any way exclude women when used to designate humanity. I have maintained Dadié's original paragraphing and end punctuation as much as possible, especially his extensive use of quotation marks and the use of the symbol

*

* *

to indicate the end of groups of paragraphs. The notes at the foot of the page are reserved for more obscure allusions or necessary explanations. I have not made notes for allusions that are easy to locate in standard reference works. The reader will notice that a number of times the indwelling animus of animistic belief has been translated as 'spirit' from the French *génie.* The word for African drums, *tam-tams,* appears several times, untranslated.

Dadié's itinerary in the U.S. was Ann Arbor, Michigan; New York; Atlanta; Chicago; Nashville; Indianapolis; New Orleans; and Washington, D.C.

ACKNOWLEDGMENTS

I gratefully acknowledge the assistance and encouragement of the following persons in the preparation of the translation: Claude Bouygues, Bernard Dadié, Richard Martin, Janis Mayes, George Stanley, and Leonard Van der Wekken. I would like to thank Karen Hatch, the reader for the University of Illinois Press, for her valuable contribution. And for the preparation of the manuscript I am grateful for the assistance of Darrell Bailie, Audrey Elliott, Ron Haukenfrers, and Rhonda Ross. With special thanks to the Bear family.

ONE WAY

ROOTS stretch, tighten, and snap. The plane has lifted off.

I'm leaving for fabulous America, country of trigger-happy cowboys, continent from which there often rises a clamor about a black man lynched for having dared to look admiringly at a white woman or about a black man forced out of a university, the mecca of intelligence—a marvelous country of backward pioneers.

I will often have occasion to contemplate that new species, the American woman, who lords it over the whitened skulls of blacks, and to realize that two rivers can share the same bed for centuries without ever mixing—a mysterious country where devils easily assume an angel's face.

Yes, I'm finally leaving but at the time when people there are preparing to hibernate. What can I do? It's the last chance and I must seize it by the toes for my hair and body have left long ago; my carnivorous mind, which jumps on events, is still embryonic. Obviously how can life be spent watching for chances, jumping on chances, hunting chances, playing wildcat, bird of prey on the lookout when fathers and mothers believed it better to develop no warlike instinct in a world where the rules call for the brotherhood waylaid on some other planet? What color will this brotherhood have when it finally reaches earth? Among the men who direct the ballet that is our daily life there is heated competition to give it one. To look very closely at this existence is to seize all its drama and to understand that there are species whose claws and fangs should be removed. Panther-men exist, more ferocious than ever in modern societies. Also hyenas, resting neither night nor day, their gluttony surpassing that of the beasts of the bush—a sign of progress, of evolution. It's sometimes frightening to admit that man has been created in the image of God, the god of business, of our armies, of our expansion, of our domination. A very ugly face! Did he not create man grudgingly? Were the day and hour he chose for this act ill-fated? In brief a face that God no longer recognizes, thus, no doubt, His extreme patience with everyone. Damn it! the Parisian cries out angrily in order to stress that man remains a damaged god, an unlucky god, cramped just about everywhere, compressed, the captive of muzzled and mutilated dreams.

America!

I'm leaving for new gods, whisked off in their modern chariot to paradise. A most pleasant trip: to go straight to the gods without passing the narrow gate of death, without sacrificing anything, eyes wide open, head teeming with dreams and plans! Death has been vanquished. The gods are on earth and men wonder what heaven is left to seek by suffering deprivations, poverty, worries, restrictions when the gods come to them, live among them, and sometimes crunch them...

I'm leaving!

"From now on turn over a new leaf. Discover the new world." The brochure coaxes me with its display of fireworks. Who could resist such an invitation? What man doesn't admire his taxes going up in multicolored smoke during one big night of celebration? When the gods are sated, people are secure, only more and more greedy and grubbing, confusing groveling with genuflecting.

"President Kennedy and the Governors of the fifty American states welcome you," the brochure continues. A global greeting which shows off the democratic character of their administration. We might wonder how a president can be put on the same level as a governor. Doubtless the power of America rests in details of this sort where sensibilities and rights are not offended. Like the tractor pulling the plow, the president slowly leads the governors and they all work together to give a human face to their country. But isn't it also democratic for me to be in the "castle of Maintenon?"[1] Whereas in Persia it's carpets that fly, whites make their castles fly. They must be happy people, well-versed in magical practices. It's no longer surprising in the least that they take all our gold without our knowledge and capriciously turn us into sleepwalkers.

I'm leaving in my castle, which the clouds respect. Still asleep, the wind does not play with the plane. From time to time we jump a small stream, bump up against a small rock, hurtle down a hillock, climb up a slope. The motors change speed but always carry us along. They also are in the image of their creator, who ceaselessly oversees them as if doubting them. He will not let them go until they can speak an intelligible language, that is speak like a man... For now even though they pull hundreds of tons, they remain machines to be overseen, just as men and peoples are overseen—machines that must produce.

1. The name of Dadié's plane.

At the first stop,[2] staying in a splendid hotel twenty kilometers from the city, I try to telephone several friends: chiefs of staff, governors, representatives, ministers. I wanted to show that I also knew important men, men who spend their days calculating the future and their nights bent over pressing problems, those privileged beings holding in their hands the fate of peoples, a fate some play with as if it were a toy. Even in this part of the world, the telephone seems disoriented and makes life difficult.

—Hello? Hello? The Office of the President please...
—What did you say?
—The Office of the President of the Republic please.
—Wait a minute.

Ten minutes go by.

—Hello. May I speak to the Office of the President?
—Who do you want?
—The Chief of Staff.
—Please hold!...

Ten more long minutes. Who wouldn't be impatient, knowing they're waiting for such an important person.

—It's about time. Is it possible, sir, to speak with someone in the Office of the President of the Republic?
—Look, not just anybody can speak to the Office of the President! Who are you?

I state my names and titles and the voice, reassured of my good intentions, answers:

—This is the Office of the President.
—Thank you... Is this the Office of the President?
—No, Defense.
—I wanted the Office of the President.
—It's not my fault if someone gave you Defense.
—What should I do to reach the Office of the President?
—Just ask for the Office of the President?
—I've been doing nothing but that for almost an hour.
—Keep trying and be patient.
—Excuse me, sir, would you please be kind enough to connect me to the Office of the President.
—You were just speaking with it.

2. Dakar, Senegal.

— No, that was Defense.
— One moment, here's the Office of the President... Hello! Hello, speak up, this is the Office of the President.
— The Office of the President?
— No, Defense. Who do you want?

The voice was harsh, full of powder, bullets, revolvers, machine guns. It was hardly the moment to lose my head or joke around. Before me, beyond the ocean, a magical America stretches out. A soldier is a modern sorcerer who kills from a distance. Behind me, my family. Reasons to be cautious and rehearse my sentences a hundred times. A weapon is an evil power, a terrible spirit, a siren whose touch charms you and increases your potential: an armed runt is worth ten giants.

— Would you please tell me if Mister A... is in...
— No, he is in the capital.
— Excuse me, and Mister K...
— In the capital on vacation.
— Well, I'm sure I could speak to Mister Y...
— He's in the capital too.
— Where did you say?
— In France.

Blessed France, whose maternal bosom protects her children so well that they're all cold once outside her enclosure. It's sometimes feared that these spoiled children might get indigestion. The worst French suits all stomachs and gives every privileged person the color and look of sparkling good health. France can claim to have touched both the heart and mind of her former subjects.

Here and there old blockhouses with rusty cannons, vestiges of the warlike fever of 1939. Doubtless there was not enough money to build schools and hospitals or to buy medicine to improve the quality of life of workers: there was enough to build these blockhouses where nearby the local people, bare-chested and bathed in sweat, laboriously scratch the earth to make peanuts grow. What beautiful images, these rusted blockhouses and these men bent over their hoe,[3] that old work tool. Progress for them means producing peanuts and in the evening rushing out to the movies to follow the adventure of cowboys in towns, on plains, or smoking a new brand of cigarette and trying a new drink. Factories produce their products for them. If happy, perhaps they

3. The French term for this is *hilaire*.

would no longer pray and therefore God would die in their heart. Still they sing, but transparently, expecting a better fate. A monotonous song, as if they were attached to the earth, chained, a sad song which sometimes flashes like a flame shooting up intermittently from a mass of smoke.

Africa is breaking her chains, but which ones? The chains of the past or those of sterile imitation? Are African states also going to pour huge sums into military expenses, allowing poverty and slums to proliferate, or by their daring and their true view of life are they going to help set another course for human relations? So Africa, at a crossroads, is breaking her chains. And some people would like to give her a stained apron and a nametag at every meeting. Elsewhere man has been confused with mass-produced goods, so perhaps it's time he has a particular label to raise him above the brute some would like him to be. Thus we would finally throw out the images of a hateful, angry, greedy, domineering, and selfish god. Another face is essential for God, not the heroic cloak-and-dagger one he has been saddled with.

A taxi speeds me toward the city, introduced by proud buildings—essential symbol of progress and civilization. By nesting so high, men hope to enlarge their vision. To the right and the left, desperately poor neighborhoods: children splash in pools that reflect hovels whose flimsy boards the first windstorm will sweep away. The dominant culture, the many tasks of the new state, the old political and economic structures, maintained and strengthened, girdling the nation—all are suffocating. Local color is a tourist necessity: traditional Africa bent over the hoe on the hovel doorstep welcomes the generous tourist who comes to observe it like a beast in the zoo. It's imperative for Africa to turn over a new leaf! Either to be Africa, a new force, a new value, not to disappoint any of the hopes placed in her, or to remain a storehouse, a granary, a market with new colors that will clatter all the more loudly in the wind to hide their weakness and be drunk with false power.

These shanties drunk with miseries, full of hungry yawns and quarreling and threatening noises, make everyone grasp the enormity of the stakes...

A change of planes. I board an American plane. It's good politics when in someone's country to be transported either by him or by his relatives. At least there is no risk of getting lost. All my baggage, including hand luggage, has been weighed. I said something. The customs official looked at me and responded: "Pan Am is very strict now." Certainly bad ideas not weighing enough have been able to penetrate the American borders enclosed in briefcases. I wanted very much to climb onto the scales to know my weight in the affairs of this strange country. I understood: you must leave for America naked in order to return better dressed. The truth is that transportation companies, having given a taste for air travel to thousands of people, are showing their true face. The smile is gone, the orientation over, out come the regulations, the law. Twenty kilos... The plane isn't made to be a moving van. A toilet kit, a lipstick is enough, and you can leave them behind since you can find them anywhere in the world. Air travel teaches us how to choose the essentials.

Most of the passengers wear suit coats with a slit up the back. This is done, it seems, to give them some flair, to show they're different from other people. I sink into a deep seat, noticing air vents and individual lights, set to do everything without disturbing my neighbor: each person is at home. Here I'm on the plane of freedom and individualism, among a world of travelers separated by seats. A woman with two feathers in her hat is reading *Reader's Digest,* a condensation of the news. From time to time a furtive smile brushes her cheeks, lingers a second on rosy cheekbones, and vanishes into thin air, only to reappear on the lips of another passenger, whose eyes shine with joy. I will later learn of thousands of examples of this jellied reading: *Football Digest, Black Digest, Gold Digest,* etc.... The second tackles the black problem directly. The booming laughter of the black man on the cover of *Black Digest* could be frightening to readers, not always sure whether he is baring his teeth in anger or from an excess of joy. In the end some people buy the magazine to examine the customs of these strange American creatures, "Everything you always wanted to know about blacks." I have yet to find a "Love Digest": could love be taboo here? Thus it will be difficult to learn how Americans grow, consume, and digest love. Could love be such a vast, large, powerful subject that it can't be reduced to jellied precepts? A Reader's Digest of the heart seems to make Americans tremble.

Our reader, like her compatriots, dislikes wasting time on details she would certainly find useless and cumbersome. Waste not! America does not seem to be a country of poets and dreamers.

Specialists prepare for their fellow citizens the minimum they must know to shine at parties and get ahead. A country in a great hurry to climb to who knows what level both in the world and in the hearts and minds of her people. A Reader's Digest! Is that not putting blinders on readers, cultivating mental sloth and killing their pregnant curiosity?

Big deals and the straight and narrow: surveyors and geometricians who for the sake of the big picture might ask you to talk about the moon in fifteen minutes. If you protest, you can hear that, although not a hard and fast rule, at the sixteenth minute, someone will check a watch, then two, then four heads will get together, finally ten, and all will convince you with unequivocal and vivid signals that it's time for the audience to change disks. In this country of intensive production, it's bad form for a person or a product to stay in the saddle for too long and risk braking or blocking the great press. What if you pretend not to understand anything of these "speaking signals" or of the deals being concluded all around you? That would never do! America was not born yesterday: the chairman brusquely rises, everyone applauds, thus cutting off any inspiration. A radical way to get rid of a speaker, a lecturer, simply turn the page or change the music while observing all the social conventions. No one prevents you from speaking; everyone rises. You can continue without bothering anyone at all.

Life jacket in her hand, a stewardess acts out a play in a national language she hopes is international. She stretches out her arms, covering her nose with a mask, as if to frighten us. In case of an accident, the death of non-American, noninsured passengers would be no great loss: when you are going to the U.S.A., you are supposed to understand the language. To be American or not to be—a new dilemma for mankind and the world. To learn the new, encroaching language or to flounder in old habits: either sprout far-reaching, heavy, and bulky wings and a halo, or be condemned to keep body and soul together, to have no clout in the contemporary world, where arms and slogans are always necessary. These people loaded with guns and rifles sometimes remind us of old highway robbers and road builders, who kill a man to take his little bit of gold or some grimy bills. Man has lost value on the exchange since he can no longer be traded and thus "his value is diminished in order to teach him how to live."

American composure is understandable: this man who plays when he should be hurrying and laughs when he should be crying has confidence in himself, that is, in his guns and the infernal power of his money, allowing him to so dominate events that he can ask you to dance or to play when fire has just broken out around you. A fire is not really a strange phenomenon, and if it destroys your furniture, you are fortuitously given the chance to renovate—a providential event that stirs things up. I suspect American merchants of reopening their doors at night when the firemen go by—an opportunity which allows them to rescue their fellow citizen by selling him new furniture, new carpets, new clothes. If you refuse to play or dance, this man will suggest something else, assuming that your means will allow you to do better and more than your neighbor—banal competition that makes the whole world turn.

At the end of the flight, the plane marks no pause. A slow people whose brusque gestures would like to make up who knows what delay, the only way they have to dominate machines, possess them, subjugate them. Brusque and authoritarian gestures of a master, a knight.

They will deliver him from the gears and confer on him the title of man, the first delicate machine created by the hands of the creator, the machine that began the development of the world. He sits astride his image and tames it.

*

* *

Lisbon! It's extremely interesting to go to America by way of Lisbon, to see people in this capital city still busy with procuring and selling ebony, living the glories and splendors of 1443. What would nations and peoples become if they didn't have in their history milestones which unite them and differentiate them from others? They all seem to be shipwrecks clinging to a drifting buoy, generations hindered in their progress bumping up against these reef-dates. Oh! how many monuments, smelling of powder and blood, should be blown up in the world! How many pages of history should be wiped clean in order to free man, to lift him out of himself, to push him toward his neighbor... In brief, on land, new caravels get ready to conquer that other ocean, the air, in order to subjugate people demanding their independence. The Portuguese river does not recede: it remains swollen, constantly alluvial. Planes have "lifted anchor" with their cargoes of soldiers.[4] Huge clouds hide them already. If they swoop down from the sky on peaceful villages, feasting or sleeping, then it's because God approves their actions. Mothers accompanied these future heroes who were going off to sow death in other homes. They all left with a smile on their lips—exterminating angels. The children of Egypt remain subject to the anger of the gods of Lisbon.

My seatmate, a charming young American woman going to the West

4. Dadié is referring to the soldiers used in Portugal's military campaign in Angola.

Indies, smiles every time she speaks to me. And she never stops talking to me. The American smile has the intoxicating power of the dollar. And the smile of my seatmate, the sparkle in her eyes, made me no longer feel the jolts with which the capricious clouds buffeted the aircraft. How is it that this woman dared to sit beside me? Very racist people who would change sidewalks at the approach of a black! She must have one of those very ordinary names: Barbara or Gloria. But Gloria seems to me to be better suited to the global ambition of America. I answered all questions and statements with "Yes." This response worked a miracle. She passes me her meal, table setting, pillow, magazines, and, at the slightest movement, says:

—How do you do?
—Yes.

And this simple word made her more maternal. I would have liked to know her language to engage in conversation, to ask her name. At least I had the "Yes," which made her smile. That seemed sufficient in this case. She spoke slowly, articulating very carefully... Yes! Strange country where women agree to hold the door open for men to precede them! She filled in my customs forms, but that will not prevent the customs officers from digging around in my bags.

American spontaneity is sometimes disconcerting: my seatmate passes me magazines, newspapers, candy.

—Where are you from?
—No!

I hesitated between the "yes" and the "no," both having equal power to cause a smile.

America must be a truly marvelous country if women smile constantly. I understand why men can be so touchy when someone looks at their mate: their attitude shows just how obtuse they are. A woman who smiles is so attractive that you can't help looking at her: she blushes so prettily that you whistle admiringly as she passes, a joyful slice of life in motion. These barbarians would make it a lynching offense, so I must be very prudent. This thought separates me from my seatmate, whom I observe from the corner of my eye. Her compatriots should have an enema every morning to clean out their bowels and enlighten their mind: they would recover their smile and, like blacks, be able to whistle in admiration at the sight of a beautiful "earth mother" hoisting spring colors. They would learn to love with their heart and not their mind.

But... can this America of "Reader's Digests" be a country of love? Is it possible to love amidst the tumult and the rush, to love deeply when you are constantly chasing time and the main chance? How can you love in a country where each person has his own fan, reading light, and easy chair?—obviously people who are uptight, quick to react, like springs ready to burst.

Flashes in the distance on our left. Below us the ocean we have been crossing for hours. Hmm! I'm relieved to see the plane escape the turbulent zone of the sky, where spirits fight with bolts of lightning. The trip will take less than eight hours. If I'm bored, think of those who, because of economic necessity, made the same voyage in irons, in filth, terror, and deprivation, braving the anger of men and the elements. How many souls walked in this immense space? How many skeletons inhabit these depths I'm flying over? How many prayers and sighs went up to God from here! A transplantation of men, producers of wealth...

Fasten your seat belt.

No smoking.

A grand finale of lights of every color, some still, others blinking, an immense fire surrounding us, an interminable field of twinkling stars into which our plane slowly dives.

NEW YORK!

The realization of an old dream: this seemed to be the end of the world. Here I am on the ground in New York. My seatmate says "bye" and disappears into a sea of passengers, demonstrating the New York style I had better learn. Planes coming and going line up for both lift-off and landing. Energy barons preside over the show. They're really there! And I'm really here in America, civilization of oil and gas, grease machines and carburetors—one all-enGulfing rhythm! Obviously Standard Oil considers itself a most enlightened enterprise. After all, aren't Standard and General Motors the most powerful businesses in the world? In well-oiled America, motorized and mechanized, planes become tramps, taxis, winged buildings. Brightly lit service stations prove that vigilant American potentates are wide-awake, fingers on the pulse of affairs. Gigantic plane-falcons majestically slide into sight, circle and salute—rendering mechanical homage to their supreme leaders.

The immigration officer gives me a brochure for foreigners, a handout showing the effigy of an eagle crowned with thirteen stars, holding in his left claw thirteen arrows and in his right an olive branch with thirteen leaves, carrying a blank banner in his beak. The entire history of America is contained in this eagle, in these thirteen arrows and stars, in this single olive branch. The banner without an inscription is an invitation to the foreigner—a historic reader's digest. The eagle's gaze and beak are striking. It's better not to talk about that in order not to offend people as peaceful as the Americans. It's not their fault if their eagle—their own image of themselves—has flashing eyes and a sizable beak. Just like states, men often see themselves incorrectly and the artist must have been hard up. Such an eagle should not stroll around everywhere because at his sight everyone protects the children like the mother hen who caught sight of the vulture's shadow.

The thirteen arrows stand for the first states that joined to free themselves from the guardianship of the Anglo-Saxon lion, which the eaglet, long since grown-up, didn't intend to support forever. The other states have not yet become adult enough to be included in the eagle's thunderbolts. For now they remain states associated with the thirteen original colonies. The number thirteen has thus become a sacred number here, so sacred that not only will people never have thirteen at a table, in a train compartment, in a plane, never thirteen wives, thirteen children, thirteen million dollars, thirteen cars, but they push the superstition to its extreme by forbidding the number thirteen in labeling floors and streets. It's said that even time is wary, understanding American reactions well enough never to produce a Friday the thirteenth. When by the nature of things the thirteenth wants to arrive on a Friday to vex or upset Americans, an eclipse occurs that day to ward off bad luck. Americans are very highly thought of in paradise—people very respectful of their traditions, attached to their values. This attitude must come from the all-important desire not to wound the pride of the states not yet attached to the thirteen arrows, states which continue to drink tea with more passion than in the time when they were living in the shadow of the British lion, for it was because of a banal question of tea or taxes that the nucleus of the States called United separated from the English crown, which was destined to have a Sisyphean task rather than coffers to deal with. Home countries have always had to worry about making their colonies work instead of their own head. Without votes in the Parliament of the Mother Country—and God knows how much whites insist on voicing them, insisting so much that they do not always have an echo—burdened by taxes, surtaxes, more taxes, contributions of all kinds, the Americans one morning for the first time in their life undressed and what did they see? Bruises—bruises that stood out too clearly on their white body—an unprecedented scandal in the history of white men. Suddenly, as if being pumped, blood rushed to their head: the British lion was treating them like slaves—them, with their European relatives and ancestors! A holy fury seized them. Then they made the blacks undress, but they had only tribal markings. No bruises! Aha! They looked each other over, head to toes, toes to head. The bruises took on gigantic forms, giggling, sticking out their tongue at them. And their blood, now very hot, kept on climbing toward the top of their head, trying to smash it under hammer blows. Were they suffering their own bruises and those of the blacks? Which ones were theirs? They had always maintained that blacks were sorcerers, some kind of devils and now there was proof all over their bodies. The extraordinary patience, the inexplicable endurance of blacks was now understandable. And when shy, peaceful men take the bit in their teeth, it's never known how far they will go: fortunately for the English, these men wanted only a little slack. But were they mature? Did they have all the executives, all the important men necessary to guide their first steps? Did they have the monies necessary for survival? The American was only thinking of his independence, more and more angry every time he looked at his body covered with bruises, while this black phenomenon slowly continued to roast in the sun, ending up with a sheen, smiling at the stars. He seemed to be waiting for who knows what hour to strike on a mysterious clock, which he would be the only one to hear, his time seeming to differ from that of the white men. The Englishman was tearing out his hair, crying "Why?" He didn't understand how a child could distance himself from his parents. His paternal heartstrings were throbbing; he exaggerated the dangers ready to assail the young American: he saw her tracked by the Gallic rooster, by the German eagle, by the Tartar bear, in short by dozens of wildcats and birds of prey. Why? The American stubbornly insisted on going his own way. But what crown lightheartedly gets rid of a brilliant gem? Difficulties sprang up and gradually, from taxes to petitions, from petitions to demonstrations, every day and every act of resistance causing their tension and anger to increase, the ancestors of today's Americans saw red. Everyone shook hands to share their fate and teach the master a lesson: he would have preferred them divided and lost no chance to bring them into conflict. When docile subjects, whose only preoccupation was producing tea, tobacco, and cotton, met in a city they call Philadelphia, it was to look for friendship, unity, brotherhood, not only among themselves but with the home country and through her, with all other men. Alas! the old paternalistic British lion was thinking only of his taxes and prestige. He hardly suspected that the head of his subjects was buzzing with bold ideas, that they were dreaming of submarines, stereos, electric light bulbs, planes to shorten distances between countries, men, and hearts. Had they fled their birthplace only to continue to undergo hardships? Were they slaves? Had each one not ended up finding his place, an honorable one, in the new society? How can you continue to be a subject tens and thousands of kilometers away from a home country when you sense rising up in you fits of independence? The old, slightly deaf lion didn't hear the rumbling of the grumblings. How much can be understood at a certain level and at a certain age?

On D-day and at H-hour, the Americans almost panicked. The filial fiber remained so strong that they no longer knew under what guise to fight the English, to throw out the Mother Country. The wind of freedom was blowing in their ears, the fragrance of independence rising to their nose. How could they sever their own umbilical cord? These braggart horse trainers finally remembered that courage and boldness were the basis of the character of the Redskins, another choice prey and target for elite marksmen; therefore some disguised themselves as Indians to burn cargos of tea. This production hardly fooled the Englishmen, who had never had anything to do with the natives. This exploit, this final affront thus lit the powder keg. It's of no importance if London, Southhampton, Liverpool are burned—they can be rebuilt. But to burn cargos of tea was going too far. The national drink! That showed not only the most absolute scorn but also the most notorious provocation. And there are acts that a national honor, made of every individual sensitivity, could not tolerate without being demeaned. The Americans, dressed up like Redskins, caught on. The British lion had an Achilles heel—the national drink! Condemning thousands of citizens to die of thirst! Such an insult could only be avenged in blood. Bad manners have terrible consequences, and so men gathered from everywhere to wring out of the American all the subversive ideas breathed in and swallowed during his stay with the Indians. And so revolution began at dawn one morning when the sun was rising, bringing its light, invigorating power, and peace to mankind, on a morning when children were preparing to play and mothers to rock their babies. Everyone was waking from a night doubtless full of beautiful dreams and schemes percolating in brains. The war interrupted some singers as if their joy offended and belittled life. This war would last seven years—as long, perplexing, and exhausting as a European war. The first bullets meticulously searched out their first victims. Indians had burned boats, and they saw only whites, but now in their path they met blacks. Taking their sneers as provocation, they bore down on them: the first killed had a provocative name—Crispus Attucks.[5] Bullets like neither opposition, nor boasting, nor very dark colors.

They're meant for joyous, dazzling scarlet-red celebrations, and what red color is more beautiful than blood red? So they swooped down on black targets and scored a bull's-eye, finding blacks crouching, gripping the earth as if to become one with that nourishing mother, to gulp a last mouthful of milk. In fact, hadn't they been the first arrivals in this land, before the "Mayflower" pilgrims? The whites were stupefied to see that black blood was red, and with no further ado, mixed their white red blood with the black red blood. Blood color wiped out distances and united the communities, each making its war: the blacks to free themselves, and the whites to protect their interests (including the blacks). Both yelled the same slogan, the same song, and fell under the same bullets. In that dramatic game of war, Virginia Dare, the first white child, an adorable girl born on Indian land, met little William Tuckers, the first black child born on the same land. But he had already changed his name as if he wanted to cut himself off from his origins. The black father inherited the custom of giving his son the name of a friend or a benefactor. Certainly he didn't want a name, as well as a color, to be a divisive factor in the fledgling community. He was, thus, already taking steps which were destined to remain misunderstood, for what can you have when you no longer have a name? This strange depersonalization caused anxiety in those who viewed askance this attempt at blackening their names: didn't they even understand that Virginia Dare and William Tuckers were meant to be united, to bring their parents closer together? Their names? Blacks had invaded and captured all of them and used them everywhere with appalling pride. There was no sense in changing names since blacks would adopt them too, so the white Wilsons and Robinsons continued to be called Wilson and Robinson, just like the blacks. Their name had become a burden, a cross for whites to bear. And all the while, they plotted their revenge. Blacks were upsetting the order of things, switching continents, changing names, customs, and clothing. It could be said that by fixing

5. Crispus Attucks, believed to be a mulatto, perhaps a runaway slave, was one of the five victims of the Boston Massacre, March 5, 1770.

themselves up with new names, they had demonstrated solidarity with those who were stealing land from the natives. The struggle against the Indians became bitter: they were savages who had to be subjugated to make way for the inundation of whites. And to ensure that no nation would come to their rescue, they were named Blackfoot, Fat Belly, Nose Hole: naturally only a mother could pity such monsters and run to help them. Everyone gazed in the mirror and felt lucky to be different from Fat Belly, whose guts were even then hanging from an American bayonet. People even prayed to support this holy war of extermination of the Redskin, that other idiot who thought it right to take on a "warlike color." Who isn't provoked by red? Since then everyone is convinced that Fat Belly, Nose Hole, and Blackfoot can be decimated or penned up, exposed as the first specimens from God's hand after he had the felicitous idea of creating intelligent, bizarre, cantankerous, jealous beings, rascals and teasers, those gluttonous children called men, whose first reflex was to kick over their traces to demonstrate that they were definitely descendants of Jupiter. Obviously, if by chance some nonblack or brown Americans have a fat belly, it's hardly atavistic, only a curable illness. This condition is rare because not only do Americans eat very little but they're always thinking of shaping up, never relaxing. They walk as if they were going into battle, constantly on guard to defend the national colors, that with the passage of time take on gigantic proportions, cast frightening shadows, and cause darkness over parts of the globe. What is essential is to know the line as well as toe the line. Which one? Everyone wonders why cliques are so powerful and party lines so diverse. Believe it or not but lines are established by eating and drinking habits: milk, scotch, candy, salad, hamburger, tea, muffins, vitamins—all because every citizen is eager to stand out without exactly breaking from either country or the motherland. Every American is of two hearts, the American heart that can be studied, operated on, remodeled, revived, and a taboo heart that links him to his motherland. Americans find themselves the children of many mothers: the father might be questionable but never the mother. But here Americans come reversing values and upsetting minds and consciences. If you can no longer be sure of your exact mother, what can you be sure of in this life? Whom can you trust? With such ancestors, could this ever be the country of loyalty, stability, or patience?

Everyone here is very resourceful in shackling his neighbor in order to free his hands to reap success. In order not to disrupt national unity, frequent parades call people into the streets: a procession of gladiators led by girls and accompanied by women. Patriotic fibers tie in with the accents of fanfare. America the happy, where everything, hyped up, is lively and bubbly: water joyously spurts from the faucet, making everything jump, a catchy, bracing joy that gets you into the swing of things. American hot water comes from who knows what volcano: it's that hot. Lights? Who would dare turn them out? Are they not jewels, gems? Fabulous country whose soil has only known two wars! The first was imposed on it by England, which held the Americans responsible for burning his majesty's ships—fatal mistake; the second, which you might call the battle of the stars, was fought to free the slaves. Already in 1863, America was integrating her blacks even before the European nations carved up Africa: there was a way to undercut Europe, whose gluttony was frightening. Developing an appetite for blacks might cause her to have designs on the whole continent: while digesting blacks, she got a whiff of that sweet morsel. It was lucky that she did because the first mouthfuls of blacks stuck in her throat, causing the current convulsive movements of a boa bothered by its victim's horns. So blacks brought the Northern Federals into conflict against the Southern Confederates: 20 stars against 13. Using blacks, Northerners wanted to constitute the "United States of America"; more used to the blacks as a valuable asset, Southerners preferred "Confederate States of America." In short they were fighting about a shape of government. But they needed stakes, an ante, a reason: blacks, who were emancipated but not really a part of the great family, all of the stars of North and South being white, were in the waiting room under observation. When war wounds were healing, how could they admit into society without even more disruption those who were the apparent cause of a painful divorce? Even if the United States of America came into being thanks to blacks, the South still snubs them and reproaches them for not defending the Confederacy like tigers. The North holds a grudge against them for who knows what reason. In stepping across the Mason-Dixon line, the South's brutality becomes polished, urbane, subtle. The South gobbles; the North tastes and then toys with its blacks, eating them slowly, exploiting them diplomatically, burying them without fanfare when they die in harness just like any citizen—doubtless from cold or hunger? But are they the only people in the world to die of cold or hunger? This attitude makes the North seem Europeanized. Besides, the racial problem in the United States has so many tiny roots that Americans, completely baffled, just allow it to grow in order to find its real root and then pull it out with a super bulldozer. They're in no hurry: let time do its work and let light enter minds and then everyone will see that America has nothing to do with the unhappiness striking her blacks. That devastating heritage comes from others, from all those adventurers who, in their leisure time, got their childish kicks from loading boatloads of blacks to be dumped like cattle on the shores of the New World. How can this dirty page of human history be whitewashed? How can a whole herd be admitted into a beautiful living room? A well-made ewe, a ram with a magnificent fleece, proves your good taste but what about these deformed and filthy sheep? Evil western fairies leaned hastily over the American cradle and poisoned her existence with a black tale. The white hurricane carried black pollen throughout the world, spread it on islands and continents, extending the domain of the black gods. For what purposes and consequences? Faced with the pesky black's vitality, Americans, who read holy scriptures, search for the reason; the world hassles, accuses, and pushes: prove you're a great power by assimilating your blacks! Let's do the job in double quick time and shut up about it. Tear this page from your history. Look at how we free ours, tingling with joy. They're singing our praises! Come on! One, two, three. But America is no longer a country that takes marching orders from others: she reads her Bible while waiting for inspiration from God and will be as patient as the Creator in order to find a solution to this black mess. Therefore when an American mentions war, he means the Civil War. The first was a revolt against the imperialism of that time and any future imperialisms. All the other wars, which Europe calls big, terrible, world, universal (because she fancies herself to be the center and core of the world), are really only little crusades to reestablish Liberty on her pedestal. Americans view them from Manhattan Island, where there is definite proof that men babble more than women: they gossip, prattle, blab, cackle, and lay tons of Easter eggs (some experts call them speeches). This Mount Sinai of the contemporary world is dominated by two Moseses who do not know which laws to bring back from their meeting with God. People live in a state of anxiety, helplessly witnessing the two bickering Lord's elect. Which one has best understood the commandments given by the Creator in sibylline language? Whose head did the Holy Spirit anoint and thus who—finally seeing with a new perspective—will have the courage to break the barriers built between men?

Above all else, the South reproaches the North for bringing foreign armies into a family quarrel and washing dirty linen in broad daylight, when, with time, a solution could have been found. This attitude has limited the South's vision and has forced it to cling desperately to segregation and throw it up as a permanent challenge to the North and its foreign legions. The South distinguishes clearly among day, night, daybreak, dawn and scandalizes the whole world because, little by little, with time and the influx of new immigrants, the glorious memory of black heroes of the Boston Massacre died out and the American black became Nose Hole, Fat Belly, and especially Blackfoot, tracked down and chased by descendants of his companions in arms and especially by new Americans in a hurry to carve out their chosen niche in the social register of famous names.

Blacks bear the weight of all the stars of the American flag. Certainly there should be at least one black star on the banner. Putting one there will be the only permanent means of reminding everyone that there are American blacks on the continent—that they have a right to exist too.

*

* *

Ever since it began strutting around the world and dictating the law, the dollar has upset and corrupted hearts and minds. It has people so stupefied that they can't grasp the significance of a man known as Silver Dollar Tabor.[6] No one remembers this character, but rumor has it that he had an opera house built and then paved the entrance with silver dollars.

Books talk of cowboys, gold and gas prospectors, oil and paper napkin barons, cement, cannon, and machine gun emperors, and political bosses, but rarely, very rarely, that strange being who provided such a good example for his compatriots already winded by their pursuit of the almighty dollar and who place the dollar or any currency above man. But poor guy, he attracted hardly any disciples! What is a man worth in relation to a dollar, a franc, gold, a diamond? What can you purchase with a man when you can no longer barter with him? What pocket can hold such a cumbersome and wriggling coin? Man has lost most of his worth since being dethroned by national currencies and

6. Horace Austin Warner Tabor (1830–99) made a fortune in silver mining and was the first mayor of Leadville, Colorado. He made many investments and contributed to civic improvements such as the Tabor Grand Opera House Dadié refers to. Colorado lieutenant govenor, then senator, Tabor later lost all his fortune. His wife, the famous Baby Jane Doe, died destitute, frozen beside the Matchless Mine.

even by coal, which has to be mined with difficulty deep underground. The effort and danger involved in acquiring something gives it value and lustre; however, a fraction of a second is all it takes to conceive a man, even by mistake, destined to become an awkward intruder, eternal child of Egypt, whose death is a blessing.

How could a simple man influence his neighbors by practicing what he preached? To be clear in my own mind about it, I asked people at random where to find a statue of Silver Dollar Tabor, one of the world's boldest men, that rare individual who dared trifle with the dollar's reign over peoples' consciences.

— Silver Dollar Tabor? Is that an American town?
— No, a famous personality.
— Are you sure he's American?
— Sure.
— What is he in—banking, insurance, the military? manufacturing?
— I don't know exactly, but he lived about a hundred years ago.
— A hundred years! My god! What about him? Why a statue? That's so long ago, we turned that page long ago...

So no one remembers the man. In America it's blasphemous to remember such a simpleton, to tout him as an example, to let him corrupt minors. He must have been "half-baked" to have indulged in such foolishness. Since Tabor's time, the advent of "tranquilizers" would prevent such futile gestures. Besides the state would not tolerate them now. What a scandal: a millionaire who squanders his fortune harms all of America and thus the whole world. But could Silver Dollar Tabor ever be in a Hall of Fame? We might expect as much since the country is so baffling in its very simplicity, its single-minded insistence on the essential in everything. A maniacal gold-loving bent leads Americans to use the same salutation, "Sincerely yours," whether writing to colleagues, officials, ministers, even the president. With this lazy-man's formula, they don't even have to think about the degree of respect due a correspondent: they also greet everyone the same way. "Etiquette books" are not popular in libraries, so, although having record sales, they have enemies among editors of similar practical, precious, and indispensable books. It's truly a pleasure to write a letter in America: "Sincerely yours" comes naturally. You see very few gnawed pencils or pens suspended in midair while someone agonizes over how to end a letter: condescend to accept my regards, I ask you to accept my regards, or please accept my regards—all these are from courtly days of yore, outmoded formulas which democratic Americans scuttled during their Atlantic passage.

In this merry-go-round, blacks are the ones who seem harassed for having created or helped to build the fortunes now crushing them. They sing to cheer themselves up and keep on keeping on. Their slow progress continues—no rest yet. From this black cloud in the white sky lightning sometimes flashes. Without blacks, who are the life of this country, it would be quieter than a cemetery, a hell where people would spend all their time studying and consulting flowcharts and reports. They still infuse energy into scrap iron and stone blocks which gather en masse to resist time and listen to the golden voices of blacks, who shake people up and toss them into the lifestream. But, as a result of so much walking, working, and singing, they're worn out and misunderstood in this world of the dollar and come to die in their neighborhood village, Harlem, where death seems the only business allowing blacks to live, judging by the impressive number of funeral homes. In America only blacks die because they lack life insurance: in the only fatal accident in the center of Harlem, the victim was a black who certainly didn't have enough dollars to pay death off. Was this person crossing the line that others were crossing but by naturalization, a total renunciation of their tradition? There he was, stretched out across the street, arms crossed as if mowed down in action. What barbed wire was he trying to escape—what concentration camp? A car equipped for a race chase cut him off at the pass. The massacre of the children of Egypt goes on through the centuries: whites have pulled off the coup of giving death a taste for black flesh. What will happen when he demands a change of diet? They will give him orientals until they find other delicacies. Are Americans thinking about all of this when they pretend to relax? It's a sad thing to be sick and die in America, where you have come to show your capabilities. You had a bet to win, an oath to keep. Thus, to die is not only to embarrass the living, to break the oath, to take a bit of earth out of production and slow down the national economy, to curtail the national ascendancy, to no longer be able to consume, to break a link in the great chain, it especially—and this is the serious part—the unpatriotic part—proves to dazed and bewildered bystanders that America is also mortal, subject to the caprices of time, weighing no more than anything else in "the hand" of destiny. Death and defeat—these ideas must not preoccupy or distract anyone. Therefore, hired mourners with a vivid imagination would have the body seated for a last farewell, and would even put a cigar between his fingers so that, in that position, the deceased can "observe" his friends for the last time: the good-bye cigar in the country where the dead do not recline but remain active for the grandeur of America. Victory over death is to have death embalmed, to remain a citizen forever apart. Taken away swiftly to the cemetery, he is privileged to be discovered intact by future archaeologists. Besides, soon America will only bury at night lest the idea of death haunt or disturb anyone. People are almost angry at those who die, treating them with scorn, as we do our hanged criminals: no mourning for them. Naturally how can earthdwellers empathize with underground residents? This ambiguity in relationships disturbs American citizens, who are worth nothing unless upright. Once stooped, their value drops, and so Americans always walk with chest expanded windward, asserting themselves against adverse forces: accepting any wager, mobilizing hundreds of warships and patrolling thousands of "miles" of personal waters for years, digging canals under the ocean, stemming the flow of rivers, canalizing and taming raging falls and making them docile playthings, being in general over six feet tall and born under a lucky star surrounded by fifty other brilliant stars—defying time and thus not expiring like a common candle the wind snuffs out. And that is why Americans bury the dead by using fourth gear of ultramodern hearses, whose discreet shape allows them not to attract the attention of passersby: no one pauses to pay last respects. It's not so for celebrities, whose fate is different, since they have succeeded in making America admired by other peoples.

America—it's life, movement, agitation, setting sail. Bitten by the fever shaking up the whole world, everyone would like to be a special case, a special cell or cyst with his own electric sign and traditions even though he's destined to melt into the sea-green ocean of crowds stopping like automatons at the Don't Walk signals.

In this electronic empire, everything has to have a purpose—the least gesture must pay off, so nothing is done at random, but only after mature reflection: waiting calmly for the elevator to return from the thirty-sixth floor is an admirable energy-saving habit. Why get upset over trifles? The elevator is like a train with timetables and destinations. To be American is to know how to keep cool in all circumstances, especially to be able to get along with the elevator, the key to modern buildings. America indulges herself in architectural daring thanks to the elevator: that machine, whose invention went unnoticed, has influenced every builder. From now on, the Tower of Babel can be built, provided with elevators and escalators. Thus, the true American is not the person who comes to make a fortune and then disappears after leaving his affairs in the hands of relatives or associates, but instead the person who, bucking winds and tides, remains at his post until the last gust, to hold high the torch of the fifty stars.

*

* *

—Have you seen the Empire State Building?
—Have you used the subway?

Everyone wants to show me the most beautiful city sights, the suburban houses and bridges, everything which by common consent seems to represent the country's best. Is this a lesson for new nations, still looking for their direction and thinking that putting up buildings is a sign of efficiency? These huge edifices seem to me like compartmentalized kennels that give their occupants a special mentality no matter where they're located: social categories are becoming floor categories. America surely is asking you to understand her way of life and not to import it, so, to discourage naive imitators and stay in first place, the flagship, everyday she demolishes ordinary buildings to make way for superbuildings. It's a sickness—the sickness of constant renewal: throw out a dress worn only two or three times, change cars every year, in other words, be like the snake that sloughs off its skin. America wants to save mankind from squalor, poverty, and all restrictions: at present the experiment only reaches a minority, those fortunate American guinea pigs whose names appear in trendy gossip columns and who search each other out everywhere. For now it would be impossible to multiply these important people: more of them would cause a traffic jam at the entrance to the only door to the fortress, the Golden Gate, which should have been in the state's coat-of-arms. However, America had the diplomatic subtlety to realize that this Golden Gate would have insulted other capitals that have gates of marble, stone, even brick. Fortunately, to save face, they all give gold keys to illustrious visitors as if to rise to the level of the country of fifty stars, laughing surreptitiously at talk of the gates of Saint-Cloud, Saint-Martin, Brandenburg, and others. Which of these famous apertures can compete with the Golden Gate, whose shape and size fills every American imagination?

People reproach American tourists for not knowing how to travel, for speeding through Europe in a week with eyes raised, looking for skyscrapers and neon lights even more lurid than their own, like hurricanes flashing through famous cities celebrated by poets and lovers. Americans do not travel to rest but to chase ideas, compare, learn, see what they can improve at home to outstrip competitors. And what they see elsewhere—stunted buildings, poor imitations of drugstores, midget supermarkets, sandwiches without cellophane, warm Coca-Cola—confirms the superiority of America's life-style. Why would others try to imitate it if America were not a genius in business and building? Wanting to give everyone elbowroom, these citizens of free America do not like to read advice on paper napkins handed to them: "have a good time, but do not break anything." How can you run a factory or be progressive without breaking something? Breaking nothing means being condemned to live sordidly, to mark time, to flounder in old muddy ruts. Living means shaking something up inside and around you... breaking a glass, a plate, even hidebound traditions, going ceaselessly forward, becoming bigger, heavier. Thus, whatever else may be said, America is the country of innovation: she intends to inject new sap into everything that has been drying up for centuries—a new spirit of dynamism: New York—New Haven—New Rochelle—New Utrecht... and finally, there's just Paris, not out of respect but embarrassment: there are so many alleys and side streets, which Parisians adore, that she no longer really knows if Descartes was French. The construction in Paris scarcely seems Cartesian, but who could have thought that the ghost of Descartes would eclipse the other august shades populating Paris? Americans, more used to the square, the level, and the plumb line—masons and architects—wonder if it might be necessary to import Descartes, not as a master of thought but as a symbol to be saved from the oblivion that is his fate in Paris.

The Golden Gate is the eye of the needle through which you have to pass, and to pass through this gate is to pledge allegiance to America. Most people pass through happily, except for some timid ones who have to be pushed into the water. For them, tunnels and immense bridges have been built, bridges rising to the level of buildings to permit the cascading flow of vehicles. A bridge opens here, another there to let a boat pass; on a third an express train slips by; a fourth spews forth trains, cars, and trucks that, from a distance, following each other so closely, look like gigantic centipedes. All this agitation showcases American vitality and boldness, and confounds other continents, because America does nothing noncompetitive. Is she not the only country to have an illuminated Statue of Liberty, the only one to accomplish this astonishing feat, the only one to join together a series of moving stars?

Observed closely, these stars seem to be good-natured guys, with arms and legs spread out, barring the way to who knows whom or what. To facilitate this role of watchman, city streets are divided into East and West by a big, neutral artery. Americans prefer the West, where prices are reasonable: they do not like to discuss the East, where the most important people live. Whether behind a river, mountains, or garden, East remains East. These two points, one seeing the sun rise, the other seeing it set, remain rivals for many people. Of course, the sun unites them in its movement from cradle to grave, but, in our day, who wants to remember that in dying we return to the place we were born? Only blacks could entertain such a backward idea. Thus it is that nations called great because of their size, the riches they have exploited, the power of their weapons, the number of soldiers they can cold-bloodily send to their deaths, and also because of their insatiable appetites, are stars fighting to illuminate the universe. Which one will dazzle us the most? Which one will draw us into its orbit? Which one will remodel us capriciously as the potter molds his clay? The only charity powerful nations seem capable of is swallowing others: people become stair steps or rungs on a ladder. The world is straining feverishly toward unity.

*

* *

It's not surprising that boxing was invented in America, since her people are always on guard to preserve the universe she is creating. Building up a world no one else is allowed to touch, she is like a soldier always mobilized to remain the model boss. America has refused to multiply political parties in order to keep things simple and clear; she thinks as little as possible so as to lessen the chances of going wrong. Few choices make the political system a *Reader's Digest.* America first observed nature, then considered man: two arms, two feet, two eyes, two ears, two jaws. One political party would be unnatural, four a monstrosity. Thus, fleeing the dictatorship of one party, one tribe, one company as well as the imperialism they fought long ago, Americans, still scarred, prefer to be Republican or Democrat. No one knows which of the two, if we make an analogy to the human body, represents the left foot or left hand, since anything left is considered sinister in America. But with each day people are realizing more and more that both right and left are indispensable in every well-constituted body.

Long ago specialists harked generations back to the story that, at the Last Judgment, God put sinners on His left, only then to lead them toward Hell. These sediments bear corrosive fruits, attracting other evil ideas we all carry about in relationships with those who differ from us. America eyes the left with vigilant distrust. The two parties evolve between the center and the right, taking turns in constituting a government with the gigantic task of holding the reins of a country whose limits spill over onto other continents. The Republicans have modestly chosen the elephant as symbol and the Democrats, out of humility, the donkey, thus publicly admitting their will to put Christ's preferred mount on the spot. A marvelous agenda! A concern to allow the poor and disinherited to have some sun, to run without being trampled, without aggressiveness, toward the banquet of life; to finally leave the slums, bidonvilles, favellas,[7] and other stinking caves, vestiges of prehistoric times. The donkey is rightly at home here in America, self-styled elixir of youth, promised land for those whom the Old World had rejected, coughed up or crushed, those whom history had mistreated, trampled, and placed out of circulation in its jolting, hobbling march or its whirlwinds—worthless derelicts that no one wants to retail as spare parts: even an antique Greek jar is more valuable. They are, nevertheless, men with flashes of dreams in their eyes and rhythms at their fingertips; their twisting and tugging guts were being obstructed—torches too brilliant in the shadows they wanted to lighten, singers of life, refusing blinders: America greeted them with open arms. But the DONKEY has gotten so fat that it seems like the golden calf, and you have to look closely to observe his long ears. This country knows how to market its products very well and only the trained eye can detect flaws. A strange household: the eagle, the donkey, and the elephant—a new mixture in that immense laboratory which is America, a country that prefers to reveal only her star-studded face to the world. The eagle also goes abroad to procure prey, taking it in such a democratic manner, with the victim's consent, that no stones can be cast. Besides, who would be so bold as to challenge an eagle crowned with fifty stars?

Parisians would search in vain here for a Saint-Denis gate, because no one here loses his head. What would be the world's fate if Americans were trigger-happy? Businessmen especially maintain a frightening calm, acutely aware of their importance in world affairs, a world they

7. European and Latin American slums. *Bidons* are the large oil drums slum dwellers use as homes.

want to save from disaster. Latter-day Saint Martins who do not intend to be fooled by appearances or carried away by feelings, they will agree to share an old coat, but only after you answer hundreds of questions about the nature of your opinions, the state of your health, the number of spouses and children you have, what caused your cavities, how strong your nerves are, etc.... They psychoanalyze you in order to offer you the appropriate tranquilizer: Coca-Cola, the dollar, or weapons. They put the bit on others and manipulate them with such dexterity that they barely feel the painful effects. To be brief, they have all the qualities of the rich and the powerful: hard of hand, hearing, and heart, they only bend in carefully chosen cases, and if you see someone close one eye and wink the other, that is only to size up an investment. American generosity is not always calculated but it's selfish, like the generosity of every great power. And that disturbs many people, who judge Americans devoid of malice.

What is even more striking in American habits is an extravagant taste for island cane sugar. No one knows why these cold-natured souls boil with righteous indignation if there is no sugar on the table: it's said to be a state secret. It's a miracle that Americans still have good, solid teeth.

*

* *

Here not enough time has passed for many names to have been engraved in stone on buildings. Breaking with the old European traditions and, showing they're really a cut above the others who are not so forward-looking, they prefer to show up on refrigerators, tires, pens, cars, telephones, carrying far and wide the flag and heraldry of new dynasties. Why be limited to several acres when they can have millions of subjects happy to live in their shadow and support them? Who can object while being wished a good and happy New Year and a long life, even if he is going two hundred kilometers an hour toward death? Goodyear! You really are a grump if you get angry at the wishes for happiness and wealth that Goodrich offers. Having decided to live according to traditional norms, America wants to be Santa Claus, no longer arriving down a smoky chimney but knocking on doors of states, the new Magus on a mechanized mount, bearing gold to all nations, smiles and urbanity bearing witness to total disinterestedness. Pro Deo!

Mastering the ocean, "jets" have reunited America with the Old World but also disturbed her sleep. She is no longer a new world but a land inhabited by old people looking for new routines. Thus hair does not turn gray but is bleached because heads are bubbling over with ideas so that factories run, the dollar hums, buildings rise, and continents creep closer together. Tense from the stress of the search for well-being, the acquisition of fortune and economic supremacy, America wants to be a huge storehouse of riches, an endless mine of everything consumed on earth. Mad, unbridled competition jumps out from counters, signs, windows; limousines with white lights, the better to see and stand out in the anonymous human flood, honk every second to indicate a presence—these luxurious vehicles have the suppleness of the tiger and the majesty of the lion. At night ahead in my path, I think I see a cemetery, a beautiful and profound lesson and healthy warning for these latter-day conquistadors: either the beautiful car and perks, or rest in obscurity. Everyone works so as not to be in the cemetery. It can be confirmed that every American is a factory working in other factories—cities—each one a piece in a giant puzzle.

Limos are in their element on avenues and between tall buildings: they fit marvelously into the national context, a context so precise that elsewhere they appear extravagant. The bird-cage-like factories are out of place among the canyons and stalagmites of New York.

Hanging onto his wheel, the taxi driver deigns to shut his door after dropping me at my hotel: I wait for him to return the change. He offers a "Thank you very much" and drives off. How can I stop him? What language does he understand? Funny country! Obviously with such business practices, who would not become a millionaire in several years! What would the driver's attitude have been if I had simply said "Thank you." He has disappeared into the long, frothing forest of red lights—all in all a beautiful sight. Later I was to learn that those who do not want to return the change all say the same thing... Here I am at the hotel. A functional room on the East Side: small bed, telephone, voluminous telephone directories, easy chair, mirror, tiny bath, and a Bible to convert me and improve my manners. Unfortunately it's written in a language I do not know, so it decorates the end table. For the same price I could have had a double room on the West Side. The battle between West and East, eternally opposed apparently, is clearly revealed in New York. America is a test tube, where chemists prepare their experiments; without leaving their lab, they can affirm and substantiate the superiority of the Western economic system over the Eastern one, which is too aristocratic and mystical. A forty-four-dollar suitcase in the East sells for half that in the West. Without even wanting to, East Side residents associate themselves with and defer to gold in all circumstances. What place does a man have in such a system? What can his future be in such an environment? What possibilities for development are offered? Can anyone be anything but a member of a herd of miners, consumers, soldiers ready to defend a citadel whose defenses are reinforced daily? Imperceptibly, the internal, domestic rivalry has transposed itself to the national level, where the East-West battle has grown to terrifying proportions, constantly threatening peace and the home of every person caught in national nets, spun of diverse and sometimes sordid interests. The honor of the West, as the sun's coffin, collides with that of the East, as its cradle. Even though the stars show up daily, no one in the two camps wants to see the evidence for fear of losing face by being more intelligent than his neighbors. So the circus goes on over the years, presidents, and generations. Witch hunts too, since, in the opinion of some people, to evolve is to espouse all their qualities and faults, flounder in the same ruts. Many Cartouches,[8] having entered and terrorized cities, consider themselves a brilliant court; therefore they have knowingly corrupted consciences, forked tongues, shrunk horizons, destroyed families, and terrified hearts. Man has been milled, ground down, and reconditioned in order to allow him to play a role honorably in a society made of an infinite multitude of spare parts, all wanting to wear the same signature, the same label. The factories know what they're doing; the people, on the other hand, have so lost their bearings that they open nursing homes for old people: youth and age are two streams that do not mix. The generations here seem to jostle each other, to take turns as new car models on the roads and in garages replace old models. America is booming and bubbling over with vitality.

There is no star at this hotel entrance to indicate a rating. The nation calculates that if you had to add up the stars of the U.S. flags, military chiefs, and planes, the universe could not contain them. Since certain countries might not have done this arithmetic, America does not feel the need to stick them on the peaceful exterior of hotels. This gigantic comet encompasses a spin-off of states and white stars, the latter the outward signs of a commitment to peace. Only the diabolical human

8. Louis-Dominique Bourguignon, also known as Cartouche (c. 1693–1721), born in Paris, was head of a band of robbers. He was broken on the wheel.

mind could have made the star the sign of military valor. The multiple white stars testify to the purity of American ideas: it's against her will that she builds cannons, rockets, giant battleships, but what else is there to amuse children who are ready to chase butterflies and other bellicose beasties? America is an old granny who knows how to lull her grandchildren to sleep with rattles of gold and the sweet breeze of the dollar. In every realm of human activity Americans would like to accomplish what Europe would have if she could have stood back, observed herself, and analyzed the results of her actions. The lack of perspective and space has condemned her to trample people and dreams, to flounder in thousands of contradictory interests, to wage war for lakes and gardens, and even when she was able to leave her borders, too much blood marked her passage. America does things more properly, more tactfully. At first glance, this country-laboratory does not seem to have a soul: nothing dominates, stands out, grabs and holds you. Instead, mountains of reinforced concrete built to defy tempests crush you—rocky crests built by who knows what cyclops. Everywhere walls, surfaces, facades which seem to want to touch the sky, veil the sun, and appropriate both: they loom up, rectilinear rivals, cities with no clear horizons, gutters full of life, movements, noise. You have to be on the top floor to have air, sun, perspective; thus, Americans have to try to reach the summit of these numerous peaks, to flee the gray walled day, to be first in a line of mountain climbers. But how many are there who can scale these vertiginous heights? So it's not surprising that numerous people here are really moles; the buildings don't let them see very far. These are people whose brain has been working feverishly ever since the day they dressed up like Indians to pick a quarrel with the English. The heart remains calm because as soon as Americans get into the rat race they no longer know how to behave, and so make huge mistakes. Taken away from figures, deprived of pen and pencil, Americans seem crippled. Tripped up, they miss the order of the day, the reinvigorating, exciting warmth of comrades in arms. And there they are, suddenly torn among the elephant, the donkey, the eagle. What costume should they adopt to attract the world audience? The elephant and the eagle are frightening, while the donkey is laughable. The goal is freedom for all, whether from West Side or East Side. Inspired by their lofty slogan, "Of the people, by the people, for the people," Americans must still fulfill the last promise on the agenda. For the people. Their fixed gaze reveals an awareness of the difficulties to be faced in winning the battle against themselves and new and old strongly overlapping feudal powers, a difficult phase which requires detailed plans, lengthy meditation, exceptional energy. Naturally, Americans are measuring their steps and taking their time in order not to proceed in the wrong direction. They need perspective and are looking for it even from their cars on expressways, where they can see far and wide.

Specific product of the land, the American car is the most visible, boisterous, and changing symbol of success, or the will to succeed. In motion or at rest, it takes up space, attracts attention, vouches for the imposing presence of the owner. It's a powerful fetish which, from time to time, devours its admirers by throwing them into ravines or rivers, victims carried by way of vassalage to other divinities. The gods have a clearer idea of their mutual relations.

*
* *

In this country of lighted honeycombs, of streaks of neon lights, Harlem tries in vain to give a little life, a little rhythm. Every evening lighted windows seem to be peeking into everyday shadows. But blacks seem fed up with being forever outsiders in America, which markets special gels to straighten detested kinky hair. From their islands, blacks wave to the Good Ship America as she passes in the distant mainstream. The nation watches and studies blacks and only opens her doors advisedly. Imagine how many factories would go bankrupt in an Afro-American boycott! And that is why blacks are carefully patronized. They're in a new Egypt awaiting their Moses and exterminating angels. But the angels of our century no longer kill innocents and the calvary of blacks goes on in their new country: they seem to be required to be a shadow of white America, a mere trickle from the white stream, an ordinary cog, spotlighted by events. It's possible, however, to suggest that American blacks are leaving their white cocoon and shoving at barriers, shocking those Americans lulled by their laughter and songs. In this country of freedom, those who have not succeeded can, unknown to anyone else, take the train at one of the one hundred sixteen platforms and leave incognito. A tumultuous ocean, where you barely notice the disappearance of the little fish, which the waves sweep into the mouth of numerous dogfish for their lunch or their dinner, preferably as "breakfast," to build up their appetite for the day. The dead of America are found either in the belly of huge whales or in the bosom of the earth. A harebrained machine makes an entire continent dance, happy to live in a constant drunkenness of illusory power. Conscious of it, America extends her tendrils everywhere, looking for foundations, bases, support. This gigantic spider spins her webs across seas and oceans, setting her traps far from her shores.

In my hotel room, no text to restrain my rights and none of those curious old-world looks which seem to see conspirators everywhere. America "eats" man, but with all the rights attached to him: she does not treat him as an artichoke, as do some states. She gobbles him up—it's more nourishing that way. No need to tell you that oysters are very popular here—fresh eggs too.

*
* *

No one in America can stray, much less get lost; everything is carefully planned to allow any idiot to find the way without disturbing a policeman. The rule of traffic is always to push ahead, following the stream of cars or people, then to turn right or left. Such simplicity is baffling to many. Even if you got lost, it would not matter: you would always wind up in America, whether on the shores of the Rhine or in Formosa, dependents of the United States of America, new vassals in the new feudalism. America is so huge and complex that hardly anyone knows her real borders. Naturally there are misunderstandings with old-fashioned neighbors who resist this powerful state that wants to be master of the planet.

The simplicity, the good-heartedness of the American, faithful reader of Voltaire, has led him to require special dances from ministers and financiers. A passage of temptation[9] would not only be badly received by people nourished on psalms but also against the principles of freedom that has united individuals and groups from every horizon in one coherent family to attempt the most beautiful experiment in the world and to demonstrate that man lives not by bread but by money. Being indigenous, American capitalism remains enlightened: it does not have the excesses, the mood swings, and demands of a capitalism that searches elsewhere for its foundations and loyal supporters, in other words vigilant guardians. This flexibility gives it its power of expansion. The steps used to choose ministers have taken new names; the Charleston, Rock and Roll, Twist, Be-bop are danced in every living room. The one

9. The *corridor de la tentation* in Voltaire's *Zadig* (1748).

who makes the fewest gestures, dances the most woodenly, and can keep secrets becomes minister, because only weighty men can hold important positions. Only giant sea turtles know how to swim in all the oceans of the world. America is the country that wants to rule over the present without losing sight of the future. She knows how to make concessions in a time when her own interests are at stake.

It's understandable that the American is not at ease when you speak to him about things that are too complicated. That causes him to think, to question both head and heart—an intolerable and untimely waste of time. Automatism causes him to write his name legibly instead of scrawling a signature. Automatism? No, rather an affirmation of his personality. What has he to fear, knowing as he does how to rule over a large part of the world? And so this excess of confidence often leads him into dead ends which he always escapes, having in hand and pocket all the trumps needed to escape even a prison guarded by the devil himself. An illegible signature is a waste of time, so the useless effort is not acceptable. Special headgear is distributed to policemen, to hold their brains in place, so they can blindly play their role since their duties can lead to useless acts and gestures. At a certain level man is not asked to reflect, to compare, to choose; society nourishes him in order to maintain certain norms which it must monitor even if exceeded. While observing policemen, sometimes you can't avoid thinking of cemetery guards, mastiffs posted in front of private property.

As soon as I pick up the receiver, a woman murmurs:
"Hello, Hotel T... Please go ahead."

No mistake, I'm still in my hotel. That reassures me and encourages me to continue the dialogue.

— Could I have the Excelsior Hotel?
— One moment please.
— Hotel Excelsior?
— One moment please.
— Yes...
— May I speak to Miss June.
— Who's speaking?
— Bernard.
— Spelling, please.

The Americans are very weak in spelling and thus take every opportunity to practice. There are so many ways to write Bernard that they prefer that you spell it so they will not be accused of having gotten it wrong. The concern for precision, for perfection, haunts every American citizen. I wonder if everyone in this country knows how to write his name. After all, they're Americans and that is enough to establish them as a new species dreaming of houses, not castles. What is clear here is the democratic spirit floating in the air. Is the lord of the manor not the man of a bygone era?

Every person is a part of his times and lives in his times. It's hardly necessary to be in a hurry about anything, no matter what; the centuries will end up giving each individual the place he deserves.

In Harlem, the policemen in shirtsleeves are veritable hedgehogs ready to attack, lined up as they are along the sidewalks with their hand on their club. What good prey blacks are! A good resonance chamber! A choice grand parade drum! In America I really am in the country of the struggle for life—the ferocious, pitiless competition of wrestling, boxing, total defeat or complete success—a billion or nothing! Anything in between verges on failure. What film director could capture the great panorama of this pitiless battle for success, a battle waged not against the elements but against others? Elsewhere people can play chess, but here they play the game of success. Did anyone leave home to become an ordinary quarter moon, a pale light? Did anyone become a naturalized American only to remain a dud?

Everything here has to rise above and escape the ordinary, to attract attention: the whole continent is a giant fireworks display. American noise has to differ from other international noises. These are not written rules but a mentality that inspires every citizen, who imbibes it with mother's milk or a bottle and continues to breathe it everywhere.

Unfortunately, the very essence of American existence, the beautiful electronic machine, sometimes breaks down. Thus, while I was sunk in half-sleep, the telephone abruptly began to ring. On the other end, a woman's voice.

—Hello, Mr. Bowdin?
—Who?
—What?
—What's that?
—Mr. Bowdin?
—Bowdin? Who's that?
—How?
—He's not here?
—Who speaking?
—Who are you?

— What?
— What?
— O.K. Go back three ahors, good-bye!

I could breathe again finally! Women rarely call the wrong number. The winded machine must have lost its head. No! With exemplary politeness, my caller listened to my French and my bursts of laughter, designed to fill in the silent gaps: she had understood. Women—marvels of understanding. She will "go back three ahors," and in "three ahors," I will be out window-shopping while someone gives her information about Mr. Bowdin.

And to think there are people who claim Americans are difficult! This woman didn't understand me, nor did I understand her. Yet we conversed for several minutes, each of us following his train of thought and then she found the solution before hanging up, her "go back." Could there be a politer way of saving the "linguistic" honor of an unknown speaker.

The sidewalks begin to wake up, to come alive, and New York to have a sweet smell. I slip into the milieu, people exchange looks with me, and smiles hover at the corner of some lips. New York rids itself of its facade of stone and ironwork in order to free its residents. But many have become stone and ironwork, darkened and rusty, almost wearing the label of a boss, the smell of a factory.

What is striking is that no one here raises his voice: everyone takes the time to say what he wants to say and whether or not you want him to, he will pursue his idea, sure as he is of contributing something new. The road to be traveled is so long, the mission with which they believe themselves invested and which they intend to accomplish so serious, that these people conserve their energy. Thus, they approach all problems with an apostle's soul. Like new saviors, they return denseness and volume to the Bible, which Europe has not understood. Unfortunately, by their excess of love and faith, the head of Christ will be placed on a homing rocket. Let Him destroy the weeds in His father's field and pluck from the sky that other blood red star which so muddles thinking that multitudes of people dazed by propaganda are forced to admit that the beautiful and pure Star of the Magi, that sign of peace and happiness, is the same color.

This young, ardent people, at the same time bold and shy, has made the thumb they like to suck the ideal measure, allowing them to construct marvelous bridges over rivers and to weave at the entrance of cities a spaghetti network of roads with the most beautiful effect. Here skyscrapers are built, houses and bridges—not castles. Lords of the manor are not native products: the climate does not seem favorable for them, so they wait for better times to line rivers with beautiful homes they admired in their childhood.

The new arrival on this continent tirelessly pursues a dream, whether eating, walking, or working. Issuing a challenge to the world, the American wants to return to each individual his intrinsic worth, the security that a fat bank account gives him. But what has all that amounted to? It's made the country a terrible jungle and enlarged immeasurably the faults imported from Europe. A hothouse where either stunted or grotesquely large plants grow. The inch seems a variable measure indeed.[10]

Absorbed in dreams of demonstrating what can be done with money, what extraordinary things can be accomplished, Americans do not even think about clothes, giving themselves away as true pioneers, ideologues. In America clothes do not always make the man. Fortunately! And if the star-spangled banner covers and shines down on Formosa, it's because there are Chinese Americans for whom a foothold must be preserved for weekend entertainment or New Year's festivities. There are also American Chinese, relatives of those Chinese, for whom Formosa is a short distance.

America, land of liberty, likes her Chinese, even if, like blacks and Puerto Ricans, they are ghettoized in deference to the principle of respect for the individual and communities. With time, integration will happen automatically and so, to mix up this still heterogeneous society, bridges, tunnels, and one ways have proliferated. To go the same way—that means to rub elbows, to communicate, empathize, support, and respect each other, to form a block, just like buildings. Examining closely the ideals animating this country, it can be said that the existence of blacks and Puerto Ricans, all those treated as by-products, is an anachronism. What good did it do to have been the first to oppose the slave trade and slavery? After her long and painful struggle, is America resting on her laurels? Is she planning a new move to astonish the world? For the moment what is clear is that America could not get her children's dreams together and so failed to be fair: maternal toward some, cruel toward others, she only unites her brood for crusades

10. A play on words. In French the word for thumb, *pouce,* is also the word for inch.

against injustices she deems necessary to combat elsewhere. Life for one category of citizens turns out to be a beautiful stepladder whose rungs are fellow citizens. Furthermore, to see, observe, and feel each other out, in the tussle of North American existence, men wear narrow-banded hats: they fight, trample, crush, and devour each other, barefaced, like civilized cannibals. Cities offer a variety of immigrants,[11] who are not always black. In the frenzy of life, the exhausted Afro-American carries the heavy and sad baggage of the uprooted and transplanted man. What he lacks is the influx of capital and fellow immigrants. He is indisputably the only citizen who never got letters from home. As for capital, he could never have any because he was making it for others. New immigrants? The situation for his race was dramatic in both the old and new countries. Under every sky, by their sweat and songs, they strived for the advent of a new system that crushed and then pounded them. Whites brought capital which flourished, and royal warrants which were exploited. The black was the grasshopper and ant for others.[12] You continue to ask for his voice and he freely offers it, realizing that one and all will wind up meeting in Manhattan Center so that America might have a more human presence, a gentler image, a more vital spirit. While awaiting this lucky day, Americans all eat desserts in order to sweeten their behavior. Freed of her European shackles, America can stretch to give each person a zest for life, energy, success. Her precious dream—the New Jerusalem she wants to build—would win Christ's seal of approval for its elimination of poverty and the institution of universal brotherhood. Only this idealistic craving could explain America's sweet tooth, fueled by galling deprivations and bitterness. Land of milk and honey and comfort—so what if it's only an illusion? What nation is not guilty of self-deceit?

*

* *

The American boss is a man with plenty of pluck, aware of his power in the world. To demonstrate this and to prove that America is the land of liberty, free competition, and free speech, he has opened the doors to products made in the glow of the red star; at present, vodka, because

11. Dadié uses the term "pièces d'Inde," the name given to blacks taken from African shores.

12. A possible allusion to La Fontaine's fable "La Cigale et la fourmi."

of its white color, has scored a big success—a clear liquid, in a clear bottle, and, therefore, no germs, no harmful ideas trapped in some nook of the container. Needless to say, if vodka had been red or even whiskey-colored, no throat would have accepted it. When ardent reds, warlike and determined to overturn the old order of the world, whiten their national drink, it means they're ready to change color. It's a first step, the only one that counts, so it's good politics to help them in their color choice, and America is actively involved by consuming white vodka. The concern with controlling eating habits has led to the creation of the cafeteria, where the customer creates his own meal, tray in hand, passing in front of dishes and choosing what pleases him. Nevertheless the American citizen in harness lashes out and sometimes refuses the blinders placed on him. Adult, used to judo and trained to fight on all fronts, he opens restaurants with Bolshevik cuisine: Soviet bread, Russian vodka—a door open to every red idea. Is this a pardon offered for that crusading outburst against the East? The great reconciliation with satellite peoples? Fortunately, when analyzed, Russian bread has no red ideas. America never sleeps or dozes, especially vigilant about viruses coming from other continents. To enter this country, which sees herself as clean as a new penny, healthy in both body and mind, you must undergo a multitude of tests and examinations. But to get out of the country, no more formalities: America considers her maladies eminently exportable. Hasn't she taken on the mission of contaminating the whole world, bending it to the whims of the bosses of New York, those new sovereigns with many vassals?

Some people complain about American bad taste, about the poor quality of some products, but they're missing the point! People no longer have any time: the rhythm of life imitates the rhythm of machines. Here is the paradox: instead of building the paradise they were seeking, they have built a hell, one more suffocating every day. They bend their own laws and agonize over numerous decisions. Perhaps all this proves that laws quickly become straitjackets for people who worship progress. Is it to fool themselves, to carry their burden more easily that Americans grow so many tentacles outside their continent, pretending to hover in order to better dominate and manage those who let themselves be caught in numerous nets? Salvaging those cadavers in order to continue the game, godlike America has assigned a time to each offspring emanating from her factories. Does she not create them in her image? Mythology talks about the marriage of gods. Could Americans escape these urges? For this dynamic boss of exceptional vitality, for this new Chrysostom,[13] a god with hands full of gold, for this Mercury sowing dollars to create tempests or calm storms, what other game is more exciting than marriage, a school of self-discipline for each partner? But where would freedom be for the individual if he had to limit and contain himself, undergo the rigors of another personality? The gods are expansive and transcend human limitations. Anyway, did people come to America to frolic under a canopied sky or to wage battle against poverty under a real sky, huge and deep? Gods do not like enclosures, frontiers: after all, doesn't the universe belong to them? This quirk of the gods is so well known that women prefer to sit on one cheek, legs folded up as if ready to jump. They're not in America to be enslaved or to lead a sordid existence either. And so, in order to indicate clearly their horror of stinginess and highlight the fundamental difference separating them from other nations, Americans display in the largest of their museums[14] an old bed given by the old British lion, just as derelict cars are left at a bend in the road to encourage prudence.

Women, who, as a rule, should have looked after the home so that America could really differ from Europe, are always at the office or behind the wheel of a car. And no man among all these American swashbucklers, these valiant modern knights who have taken over for the angels with flaming swords aimed at the four cardinal points, no one among these noble warriors whispers to her to stay "home." They're all afraid she might revolt like those colonial women. As a matter of fact, men remember as if it were yesterday what they call the "skirt uprising" of 1760. Tired of eating Indian corn, American wives went on strike, then declared war on men and victoriously repulsed all their assaults—a stinging defeat imprinted on the consciousness of every solid American and a terrifying weapon with which women threaten men ceaselessly! That rebellion turned out to be the remote but not apparent cause of the Revolution, because Americans needed money to maintain wives who had not come to America just to keep on eating gruel. It's now understandable why money exercises its domin-

13. Saint John Chrysostom (344–407), one of the Fathers of the Church and patriarch of Constantinople, was famous for his eloquence, thus the surname "golden mouthed." Because of his concern for the needy and oppressed, he denounced the excesses of the wealthy and insisted on almsgiving. He was persecuted by the empress Eudoxia.

14. This refers to the Metropolitan Museum of Art at 5th Avenue and 82d Street in New York, which has in its collection Marie Antoinette's daybed from Versailles, as designed by Jean-Baptiste-Claude Sené.

ion and why individuals kill themselves serving it: men insist on giving their wives a heart of gold. What else can be given to wives in the country of lucky strikes.

American women in the office and on the roads! Obviously if they remained at home to take care of the children they should produce every year for a smoothly rising demographic curve, what would happen to the need for change in a United States of America, where "renewal" is the order of the day? The American people are continuing the molting process, fiddling around with the warp and woof of their threads. Men settle temporarily for a slit and two flaps on their jacket backs and women for a hat which looks like a designer's first attempt. While the American boss hesitates over the cut of his own clothes, he hastens to educate the taste of those who live in his shadow: therefore, jeans, cowboy outfits for kids, military uniforms for adults, westerns, skyscrapers, chewing gum, the sadistic pleasure of cops who think K.O. with the billy-club—haven't all these customs gleefully crossed every border? Slowly but surely, without its knowledge, the world is becoming Americanized.

*
* *

America is not everyone's Eldorado; if she spoils some, she disappoints others, and confuses the majority who can't manage the transplant of an "American skin" in order to take the pulse and temperature of fifty stars clumped together as a lone planet dragging in her wake a spray of more or less illuminated satellites. She plays so many games so swiftly and sneakily that she has become a frivolous dilettante. You court her to learn some secrets and wake up either lover or enemy, depending on her good graces, her technique, or her scent. It's easy to be mesmerized by her charms. But back to your senses, you can observe closely her hands and tell that she still does domestic work: even with washer-dryers, paper-thin pocket calculators, and change machines, America still can't totally free people from certain tasks. She has yet to invent Big Brother, the robot's robot.

It must be acknowledged that the venerable nations, the godparents hovering over the infant America's cradle, were not always good fairies. Old and wrinkled but not yet toothless, they resented her beauty, virility, and vitality. Merry Olde England especially deserves to have a guilty conscience because of its New Year's gift—an old, ratty piece of velvet cloth. All those Americans—little terrors, adventurers, seekers of sun, air, and freedom—got the point. They frequent white sales and, if a kid acts up, they drag him or her to the New York museum[15] to see the English gift. There they offer the kid a choice: the dollar or the threadbare velvet cloth. Invariably, the youngster will opt for the dollar. This is the acid test, where American parents sniff out their own true blue blood, irrigating fields of dollar trees.

The dollar is, above all, a good and holy currency, whose motto proclaims the faith of an entire nation: "In God we trust"—a currency serving the Lord. Laundered by this motto, Judas Iscariot's thirty denarii would be welcomed into any cash register; even Saint Peter could not complain. With such a bold motto, this currency must be terrifically strong, generous yet forceful. And Rome, which also has a lease in America, can only give its blessing. The dollar lacks the evil or perfidious smell of other currencies: Christ would have instituted it if only the clarity of His ideas had not so dazzled everyone that He had too little time. Such a holy currency has universal pretensions. "In God we trust."

Yes, some might call Americans naive because they take the Bible up on its challenge that it's easier for a camel than a rich man to pass through the eye of a needle. But they will make it, even loaded down with all the safes of their totem, the Empire State Building. For these contemporary men must be up to date as they mold other peoples' futures in their own image with the rallying cry: "Let all nations come to us for a new Sermon on the Mount." Their magnificent obsession is to unify men, and they pursue this dream relentlessly. And so they do not enjoy life in spite of their colossal fortune, which they do not hoard: urban, not rural, urbane, not provincial, the success of a few plunges others into an infernal rat race. Although deafened by noise, Americans rush headlong into the fray, seizing every opportunity, maneuvering in the economy by the seat of their pants—all volunteer national guards mobilized to protect that complex closed circuit maze of American life, always susceptible to the whims of a crank circuit breaker.

Neon signs with dazzling letters are all designed to attract attention, promote competition, scream success, and prove that any man given a fair chance can win in the race. America judges on actual evidence: individual talents and gifts are more important than the pedigree of a

15. The Metropolitan Museum of Art.

diploma. But such rational use of ability results in haste: cold-plate specials wolfed hurriedly at a table the help is too busy to wipe. In this gigantic factory you eat in self-defense, just to keep working, just as motors get oil and gas! Efficiency first! In some places steamy streets resemble volcanoes as all America boils with productive fever.

Wall Street! However, the fabled wall has crumbled under the weight of hunger and thirst. Well-lighted, on full display, it no longer divides men. New York has subdued, enslaved, defanged, emasculated, and leashed gold and the wall, walking them in public, obeying the Mormon principle: "Gold only exists to pave roads, saints to make the fields green." And yet very few people remember Silver Dollar Tabor. Outlaws, who sometimes attack the Wall, get caught and put away for a hundred years: America will not tolerate such incompetent failed adventurism. The wizards of Wall Street, like African wise men, are masters of tradition, rainmakers, magicians, our modern miracle-workers. Our wise men could sacrifice themselves for their people, so I suppose there are similar sages in America, an astrologer's paradise. Who better than Americans could study the stars, especially when providence no longer has any secrets? Hobnobbing with the gods requires strict manners, allows no gate crashers, so Americans do not fidget at red lights, do not sell alcohol before the last church service ends on Sunday, do not open bars and liquor stores on voting day, when they choose candidates soberly, free of all pressures from drafts.[16] To deliberately fool onself is quintessentially American.

*

* *

Large-scale corruption has made its way into the world of things, which pace themselves to please their human masters. The subway turnstile must have its ten or twenty cents to turn and let you pass; the fruit juice or quarter of a chicken must have the required coin to come out of its windowed cage. American citizens confront machines, which do not reason: standing there face to face they can see their own reflection, know what they're becoming. Their tears, thirst, hunger do not touch the Machine. Vigilant guardian of its contents, it obeys instructions. Forward sentinel—deaf, blind, and unsympathetic, it speaks

16. One of Dadié's plays on words, here *pression,* with the double meaning of beer *sous pression* and political pressure.

an incomprehensible language. Do you have the right change? Then with maddening indifference, and a haughty gesture, it pushes out before your nose, grudgingly, the juice or the quarter chicken. Next customer! It has not yet been programmed to joke, smile, or argue. That would be a waste of time. A machine doesn't smile; it functions, earns a day's pay, just like the busboy or the waitress. Not one has a smile: all the same type—all machines. "In God we trust!"

It may be, as rumor has it, that America has no past, but by her insistent assault on the present, hasn't she converted passionate followers to believe in buildings, boxing, television, khaki? What modern parade would get off the ground without American arms and uniforms? America is at peace, yet she is surrounded by barbed-wire states, by peoples by way of chevaux-de-frise. You would think that she is self-conscious about her unstable foundations as she faces the coming tidal wave from abroad. Metropolis, command post, Vatican, she is horrified by war, thus only toys with it as a hothouse experiment. Is this not the era of undeclared wars? And what better measure to prevent the button being pushed than to keep your finger nearby, ever ready. What perfume is more heady than rocket fuel? Mars, god of war, seems reluctant to stand up, so in order to keep the peace, America keeps "stockpiles" she can lend needy rebels—if there is the worthy cause of self-determination. America an imperialist? No way! Look at the map and see how her own domain is too large to encircle. She guffaws at enthusiastic accounts of the Tour de France. She conjures up visions of her race tracks and wonders what freaks would want to circle Manhattan Island at a mere crawl. A ridiculous contest with no big prize money. A Tour de France for jets lasting several minutes would make sense because it would set a record, one with technical flair. In this country of hares, snails and tortoises can't live. America wants to shock the stagnant world-jalopy out of the rut where it's mired. The American Prince and Sleeping Beauty. But the world is so large, so diverse, so volatile, with such complicated people that America wonders sometimes if hers is the way to their hearts.

* * *

What Americans want, one of their character traits, is to get back in contact with the mother country, to tie in again with tradition, while all the while remaining American; to link their dynamism and audacity to the values of the past, to join two continents and give the world of tomorrow an appropriate image. They want to be champions in this domain. In the likeness of future man the American is an uprooted person looking for new values to ground him; he tries to go to the moon because he no longer feels any ties with the earth, now poised to move back into the hands of peace-loving peoples, doubtless to blacks, who need a solid platform to express their exuberance. Like a wedge embedded in the side of white society, American blacks each day enlarge the opening. In order to maintain the racial mixture of American people, dressmakers dress them, cooks feed them, and women make them walk—all the same way. Content to live at the same pace, to exist in the same pattern, all these citizens reach out to give a hand, to help each other make the light from the fifty stars more dazzling since the light from the torch which Liberty flourishes is now faint and fading. Its role was to light up the entrance of the Golden Gate and lead boats into the channel. This giant goddess watched over New York and gave her blessing to every immigrant. Now there are airplanes, so you can enter this country without ever suspecting there is the figure of Liberty on a statue, kept for tradition as a good, old fetish. Gift of France, dethroned by Boeings and the world's tallest building, the Empire State Building, classified among historical monuments, Liberty in America has become a curiosity. Hasn't she lost face beside new structures? Nevertheless she stoically continues to brandish her torch, which no storm can extinguish. Having become a country without walls, America no longer sleeps: she can't decide what product to push to save the friends around her as well as keep their friendship. Europe laughs sheepishly as she thinks of everything that could have been eliminated; war, ideological or racial, no longer interests her. With age and experience, hasn't she lost her fervor and crusading faith? From now on, who will fight for God?

"I will!" America answers, sending forth her Bible battalions to scout out the entire world.

It's clear how much America has lacked Joan of Arcs to listen to voices and tell her what to do and how! But angels only consort with the pure and simple in spirit, with innocents. And America has rounded the capes too rapidly, without sufficient time spent in the company of the gods of her forests and mountains. The roar of machines has too soon muffled her hearing. The kings of oil and gas, cigars and Coke, and all their ilk who have toppled the landed gentry are waiting to be led to Reims to be anointed with holy oil. Now, they're almost all protestants, and it's to protest the curse on gold that they have engraved on their pennies the liberating slogan: "In God we trust." Moreover, to hasten the reconciliation among diverse beliefs, have they not sent for, who knows how, and placed in one of their museums the monumental gate of the Church of Valladolid and several old flags worn by faith, faded by tears, frayed by sighs, eaten by time and moths? They jealously watch over these hostages, these trophies, these treasures, re-creating in their country the setting their culture is missing. The skeptical tourist wonders how men could take this gate from the usually suspicious Spanish without their knowledge. A true stroke of genius, one revealing American maturity in business matters.

If, in this accumulation of riches, they were lucky with France, which gave them Marie-Antoinette's almost-intact bed,[17] quashing, thus, the French reputation for playing around—a presentable and still usable bed—they seem to have been duped by England. The English are accused of fierce conservatism, but who could have supposed it would extend to the velvet coverings of royal beds? Anglo-Saxon stinginess explodes in broad daylight and the Americans, having a different idea of economics, focus on this bed as if to explain the reasons for the War of Independence. The French no longer seem to be competitors at heart; they're now short of breath. And in the terrible race to endure, France's honor is safe and it shows, royal proof in support of the fact, that in the long run, living fully proves to be very efficient; kissing becomes a strong tranquilizer and sleeping pill. The old British lion has beaten the rooster on his own turf, and the Americans remain divided, but in our world who is not divided by the Money Wall where generations of unfortunate men are dying, their prayers unanswered? And in order not to be among this already impressive number, Americans have preferred to subjugate the Wall, to be its uncontested master, thus augmenting their prestige in the world. Everyone will know them from now on as devils but devils able to have human reactions, democratic ideas; for example, to acquire Old Masters, they will ask questions to ascertain whether the investment is profitable. This democratic idea of running the affairs of the country constitutes the basis of the expressive American vitality. America is the product neither of a man nor of a caste, but the property of powerful anonymous interest groups of unlimited responsibility. As a result of not having penetrated to this core of the American soul, newspapers can publish announcements like this:

17. See note 14.

"Enjoy being strong the American way! The American Institute gives muscles." Muscles, brutality, strength—that is America for many people. We must recognize that Americans, caught up in who knows what way with their westerns, do nothing to "whitewash" the image of their country; they keep the hideous mask in order to frighten who knows whom. The role of westerns is to reveal the American to himself, stark naked, to help him in his climb toward perfection, to give him arguments with which he must convince his wife of the necessity for them to be model-bosses. He knows that his intentions are misunderstood by some, misinterpreted by others, knowingly deformed by many not yet brainwashed by propaganda. There are tourists arriving who think that the gun always has the last word in this country of pioneers. Therefore, to mellow their behavior, restaurants serve all sorts of varieties of grass. America asks foreigners to graze and to learn how to ruminate, to help them wipe out the bad seeds.[18] This is the first ordeal, the first test, and it is recorded by radar hidden everywhere.

*

* *

If America fills its coffers with gold and then hands it out around the world, it is for moral reasons; in democratizing the precious metal, her towers can rise ever higher in the sky. Frequent scripture readings exorcise the evil genie in gold. But the devil is quarantined, because Americans, who build Empire State Buildings, surround themselves with clouds, and dominate the highest summits, can't brook any rival. And so they beat the devil, tamed him, and collared him on the One Way, which forbids traffic jams, debates, quarrels, divorces. Laboratory-tested on roads, in hearts and minds, the One Way has become "the American Way of Life," which cautions kids on beaches to build castles of solid materials on America's rocky, solid terrain—never dreamy castles in traditional, desolate Spain.[19] The American Way of Life displays a propensity for meetings, roundtable talks, conventions —in short, public relations. Gone is all sense of isolation when Madison

18. Dadié refers to the abundance of salad; eating so much salad might lead to helping America to weed.

19. The expression *to build castles in Spain* has the connotation of dreams without substance.

Avenue arrives loaded with documents, smiles, Esso Extra, Coca-Cola, and bags stuffed with endless questionnaires. Esso Extra revs you up; Coca-Cola drowns fatigue, and the questionnaires seek to reveal whether you are a safe enough risk to join the great American family, whether you can be offered a fraternal handshake, or counted on as a reliable companion on the One Way! Disgruntled, superficial people mention assembly lines. They're wrong. Such lines are for machines, which require a vast network to run them, and Americans staunchly assert their mastery over machines. At present they're all cooperating in the task, so worshipful and respectful that when the minor god Elevator is working, they meditate, waiting to take over when it's winded: here men and machines live in perfect symbiotic rapport, dedicated to the grandeur of the United States of America, dreading the eventual counteroffensive by Redskins tired of being bottled up in reservations. Their rebellious, warlike protests often shake up Americans, who ceaselessly scan the horizon from watchpost fortresses disguised as office buildings. The unlucky Redskins have yet to understand what makes the American tick—recurring anxiety about brotherhood. They have not yet understood that this noble citizen put them on the reservation to spare them certain plagues of civilization, so they could witness America's future stupefying progress. This concern with brotherhood has caused the average American to introduce himself immediately, place his nameplate on his desk, even pin nametags on his chest. In taxis you know who you're dealing with: an i.d. card is posted. Anonymity seems nonexistent as are insults. Having the courage of their convictions, Americans can face others, aware of their value, of what the world owes them—new warlords extending a horn of plenty to vassals. On the telephone, as soon as the receiver is off the hook, you hear at the other end: "Hello, Smith or Jones here..." With the enthusiastic bounce of a kid, Americans insist that you use their first name from the first day of meeting. So friendly! Expert at breaking the ice at mixers, they want to build a bridge between hearts, decorate in their favorite color, and throw a big party there where all men will mix and mingle just as they did long ago on the Pont d'Avignon—joy in factories and cities, universal joy! Poor, outclassed Saint Peter must literally shuttle Americans into Heaven. What can this god-fearing holy man do when Americans tip one side of his scale of Justice with the good book and money engraved with "In God We Trust"? What crime is not expiated by that slogan? What people on earth oozes so much faith and confidence in God? Who does not succumb to this terrific logic: "sure, I'm a sinner but I have confidence in God! And it's because I have confidence in Him that I'm so great!" A most beautiful confession! This citizen is not even a prodigal son for whom God will have to make a sacrifice. No, America has merely tried to change the face of the earth and alter consciousnesses by giving men a different mentality and identical tastes. In this fantastic struggle, she has waved her greenbacks like a shield, carrying the American profession of faith into the most remote corners of the planet. This courageous superman has shown God the proof of his trials and tribulations, the record of his errors: a blessed currency carrying peace on earth, stars followed by new magi.

Gloria in excelsis Deo.

Oh sure America is open to much criticism, notably for putting her foot in her mouth. She blunders in the adult, very civilized "My-father-says-to-tell-you-he's-sound-asleep" manner. But has everyone not behaved the same way?

After all, what does America have to hide from the world, with her citizens living in honeycombs for all to see, high on modern Sinais? Such housing produces a fishbowl mentality, somewhat off-putting of course, but Americans are so sure they're on the right track that they have put the president in the White House, where everything happens in broad daylight, as if on television. No black room in any office or apartment because there is nothing to show. Wait a minute! It's not that there is nothing to show, just that blacks have not yet defined a program of action. No one knows what blacks want in this great human and mechanical complex called America. Are they African? American? Both? Which characteristics stand out? Why do they persist in keeping their color, and other distinguishing anti-American traits? Let them slough off their skin and scrub their brain before entering the inner sanctum. No dyed-in-the-wool, true-blue American can come out black or red. These color slipups can be easily corrected by widely distributed products if you want to cross the color barrier, the pure line, the open sesame to privilege in our world. Elsewhere they naturalize, that is, dignify your color, lighten the situation a bit by a document to be perused at leisure, but in America, you must really be white. But hypocrisy in America does have limits. These primitive people thrash around in a web of multiple contradictions, lost in a labyrinth of thought processes, confused by fence-straddling, and compounding problems, both approaching and avoiding the women they no longer understand: they flock to doctors who make them feel better, as if propping up wilted tender plants! These practitioners are genuine healers like ours, who hear confessions, but, to set herself apart from us, America has named her healers psychiatrists —that sounds more civilized, more mysterious.

*
* *

The American is the upright man who thinks the same way he walks, in long strides, works the way he drives his car, quickly. Meandering throws him off, footpaths bore him, details burden him, small talk irritates him. He is the man who never asks how much something might be worth but how much it's worth. He prefers what is present and concrete. If he happens to leave this royal way, it's the fault of offices that do not succeed in getting in tune with human relations. He suffers because of this but will do nothing so as not to upset the order of things, so great is his respect for institutions whose sheen he would like to heighten but which only time can give to old age. This man has everything to be happy in the new Eden, but, advised by who knows what new serpent, continues to eat apples in permanent defiance of divine law; this man thus remains disturbed because East Siders had the gall to give their president the initial of the one in the West. Forever puzzling to the experts, nature creates these connections, obstinately wanting to maintain men and nations on the same level, house them in the same boat, while laughing at their castles and fortunes, the color of their ideas, the intensity of their faith, the shape of their heads and jaws—those enormous, insurmountable differences which clearly divide men. When Mr. K is mentioned, the American citizen has to figure out which K[20] is meant—a loss of precious time for him. When the radio announces that President K has had an attack, from two sides of the ocean prayers—white and red—go up to God. Americans do not get overly upset because they know that gorilla-bodyguards have been trained to watch over their K, who considers them jailers who refuse to give him an inch. They're afraid he will make a wrong move. The people treat them well in order to prevent them from "eating" the president.

The planes, the lights, the impressive number of cars, the women changing clothes every morning, the buildings, the different smiles had me fooled. These gorillas reveal an important aspect of America's

20. Dadié refers to John F. Kennedy and Nikita Khrushchev.

strange multifaceted image. Just think! The American citizen has scarcely evolved if he is still at the level of a brute ape. But who in our era doesn't want to tailor his customs to the American pattern? Who doesn't want to pass as an American? And so the necessity for gorillas crossed the seas and took hold in the presidential residences of other continents. The elephant, the eagle, the donkey, the rooster, the lion, the gorilla—no one really knows any longer what vulture or beast to imitate. Isolation is such a heavy burden that everyone is looking for roots, a family. Divisions among peoples seem to come from the image they do not manage to make of themselves in relation to the birds and the beasts; the human struggle is a rivalry among birds and beasts of prey, nothing more!

*

* *

Here people walk; they don't lie down on the job. No one can dawdle or lean on a balcony to observe the passing flow. It's bad taste to be out of sync, different, so there is a ban on terraces at cafés and restaurants. The example of people relaxing would be contagious. America—a terrible jungle, where you arrive hungry, thirsty, outraged, in a hurry to be established, where a profusion of artificial flowers demonstrates that no one has time to cope with the whims of the seasons. The Good Lord can keep rain and sunshine, springs and winters; as for flowers, factories can produce equally beautiful and delicate ones. Americans don't want to owe Him anything. America? A great emporium with the windows full of plastic, nylon, rayon, paper plates. Has this country not started a deadly race against the clock? What else can she spew from her multifarious factories? No savers of candle butts here! Everything is done against the clock, with ostentation, and so we have products which sometimes lack the finesse required by staid customers. America caters to conspicuous consumption because she never intends to bridle her galloping machines.

In old-world feuds, the American often plays the role of the "bad son" or the "courageous son" of our folktales, the one who always comes to the rescue of his elders when they're under threat from local ogres, the one who, after his victory, lets everyone know that without him... The elders react first with effusive praise, putting him on a pedestal, but little by little they shun him. This brave, modern warrior makes such uncivilized gestures that people do not trust him with anything valuable, fearing for their rug, furnishings, and heirlooms every time he darkens their door. But he is at ease and makes himself perfectly at home, only wishing he could redecorate so that the wise old walls couldn't talk. Their words would fall on ears deafened by the constant barrage of noisy printing presses and bulldozers. Having become a new breed of elephant or buffalo, he so dismays and puzzles his elders that one morning during breakfast his suitcase appears beside his chair. Wondering if he has made some gaffe, like forgetting to introduce himself, he rattles off his superlative credentials:

"The world's largest statue, longest river, and tallest peak are all in my country.

I myself am the king of oil, rubber, corned-beef, butter, motels, electricity, ice, and, naturally, refrigerators. A real blessing to millions of people, I'm the new magic ingredient..."

Europeans mock the royal pretensions of a monarch whose kingdom consists of stomachs and machines. Lacking castles, crown, and bloodline, armed with rails, cotton, and paper, a king who prefers to be called Bob or Tony is a laughing stock.

Still he continues his litany "From Waterloo, Maine, Milan, Vincennes, Florence, Frankfort, Paris, Granada, Rome, Berlin, Gloucester, Syracuse, Saint Petersburg, Bismark, Odessa, Memphis, and Philadelphia, home of the venerated Liberty Bell—I'm a republican king, a democratic king!"

A shrewd and prudent Europe can't suppress her snickers listening wide-eyed to so many references. Counting on gnarled peasant fingers privy to the secrets of the universe, she mutters in echo:

"Odessa, Waterloo, Bismark! What can I do with this kid? Where did he come from? Syracuse... Berlin... !"

"I have the biggest cannons in the world, the biggest planes, the latest factories. Everything sets the scale for the century: gigantic."

Europe suddenly finds that this intruder is crowding her, having outgrown all conventional chairs, beds, rooms, doors. Accustomed to having his way from his earliest youth, he now lounges around in what is called here his transatlantic chair, feet up on his table. No one can understand that a man can release his excess energy by hoisting his feet up on the furniture. Etiquette books do not yet mention this posture.

— This American is nice, but finally...
— Right. It has been long enough since the war. Why doesn't he leave if he was so happy at home?

— Our cuisine is too good! He's putting on weight. Look how healthy he looks.
— If he has his way, well-known glutton that he is, he'll just gobble us up.
— Really now, what good has he done for us?

So they try again. One morning during, a friendly chat, they nudge him toward the exit. When some scruffy passersby yell, "Go home," the American, amazed they can speak his mother tongue so well, gives a friendly wave. He knows ignorant foreigners do not know that his forebears were among those two hundred Mayflower pilgrims who, in September 1620, fled the one official way to talk to God. Thus it is only by accident that he is a tobacco king because tobacco was already cultivated in America in 1617. Don't blame him either for any neighbors who are trying to turn his state black; Dutch warships brought the first thirty slaves to America in the same year young English virgins were sold to Virginia planters. He can recount perfectly his long, sad, glorious history. During the War for Independence, thirty-five thousand women, both blacks and whites, were even used to shore up the sputtering British fighters, whose defeat they hastened. Blacks are nothing out of the ordinary for the Americans: who doesn't know that Central Park links Harlem with white neighborhoods? Still, some throw segregation up to them, but who hasn't known black neighborhoods? Who hasn't hidden behind his color? Granted, in Louisiana there existed Congo Square, where blacks got together to dance; but today it's Beauregard Square. In the same fashion, don't all Americans have the same names: Jackson, Barge, Lewis, Hampton?—the same make and style in cars and houses? Aren't blacks the best athletes and singers, so well established in America that they can be as stubborn with whites as they are on remaining black. And their vote is so important that they can screech at the slightest offense. Touchy and unassimilated, with a simple change of color these Americans would be welcomed with open arms into the flock. But why stir up such a deeply convoluted, illustrious history as that of the United States of America?

— Go home! troublemakers continue to shout around the beleaguered American.

Can America gain a foothold on the old continent, searching for a way to regain her equilibrium? No one seems willing any longer to beg and buy the right to live from anyone else: will monopolistic businesses be able to withstand the upsurge of men convinced their time has come for a place in the sun.

*
* *

Both male and female escapees from paralyzing old-world rigidity still seem to be camping out. They use paper napkins; the laundry would not dry if they had to break camp early to move on to a new destination. Anxious and uncertain about the future, misunderstood by their mates, women in the streets rarely smile, immune to all breezy currents and glances ricocheting off them. What can these automats be looking for as they scan the horizon and make a mad dash toward an elusive, doubtlessly inaccessible promise? Is America not the fulfillment of every dream? Oh! If only we could join hands in this search, we would draw together hearts of all colors. Judging by their proud bearing, their bright designer clothes, American women seem to be well-tended blooms, yet might they not long to be simply women and not American women always weighed down by a crown of fifty twinkling stars? Some of these American women are so lazy they lack even the strength to open their mouth when they speak. Could that exertion be illegal as it's illegal to have more than two hundred persons in certain rooms at the "zoo"? This lack of precision inspires reflection when you find yourself in the cell of the ancestors: Gorilla, Monkey, Buffalo, or Elephant. They point to themselves, then to you... they signal you, then, scornfully, they turn away because you have degenerated, you no longer understand their primitive language. Quick to anger, the restless chimpanzee would like to get out to ask two questions in plain language, the one to which the world's police have accustomed men. As for Americans, with their usual flair, their business and people sense, they have succeeded in understanding his speech whose essence they have translated with the goal of popularizing it: "O.K." We had to have men of the New World to link us more closely to our brother chimpanzee. And to think there are people who say that the Americans don't have their feet firmly planted on the ground! Must we deduce that the human species is still full of larvae obstinately fleeing the light which is too dazzling for them? Thus, the Americans shamelessly exploit the situation, the privileged monopoly, so much that to take any airplane whatsoever to any country whatsoever in the world, it's necessary to have what is called hiccoughs. How can you fly like a bird if you can't remember your simian origins? if you don't feel yourself in solidarity with every living thing in nature? Is living not a pact? America doesn't ask anyone to understand the chimpanzee language—one experiment does the trick; she has translated it, "reconditioned" if for everyone: O.K. With this password, all the frontiers of the universe have been removed. Finally, by means of animal language, men become conscious of their common origin. America would only like to be recognized for her gigantic effort to seize some scraps of this caged ancestor's speech in order to demonstrate the progress made since severing the umbilical cord.

*
* *

Standing in self-service lines to take a plate and grab lunch, women must be angry at men who brought them here in the name of democracy: gallantry is under siege in this prematurely aged country, doubtless shrunken by several of its transformations, where no one speaks for free, only for profit. The rat race turns out to be brutally cruel because new instincts come along yearly to relieve those that have dozed off. And in this shadowy jungle, the American woman is a true fortress—judging by everything the stores offer her as protection. She can fall only if the interior has been undermined for a long time; she can't be captured by direct attack: no chariot, tank, Trojan horse, perhaps not even Saint George's cavalry could prevail against her, a woman admirably fortified from head to toes. The most prominent parts also have their shield and their bumpers: you never know how to approach her or win her. It suffices for her to mention mental cruelty in some places for every pious soul to fly to her rescue and every scale of justice bend at her feet. However, this is a precious weapon she does not always like to brandish because, in spite of everything, she is looking for a friend, an ally, a companion, a husband. Solitude is so thick in these honeycombs that the presence of a friend, a partner, is a gift from heaven: even while at the wheel of their car, women are searching for a faithful companion, a man who is really a man. But it happens that this dear other half is thrown out of love's circuit, so he also gets behind the wheel of his car and escapes to the highway to prove that he has passed a turning point—love's disappointments and sufferings. Stingy, he runs toward other sweet chains. Happy butterflies! To exorcise this evil that corrodes society, to retighten conjugal bonds, to commemorate the revolution of the period, modern buildings are adorned with balconies: the hour of idle chatter is finally beginning for America. Tomorrow you will see flourishing salons, conducted by women in order to refine their men and ask them to devote more time to dreaming, love, and natural flowers than to the statistical curve. All that will be very easy because Americans, open to every wind and gust, aren't sticklers for anything. As proof, notice that the large majority of men on horseback in public places are foreigners, kept through diplomatic courtesy, on hold, because, one day, these decrepit men will have to vacate the squares; in the jet age, the horse can rest. Let's not overlook the fact that America is fighting with all her strength against a backward mentality which promotes capering on a horse. In no case does the bargaining spirit lose its rights, and publicity has set up shop in the subway as well as in taxis, where you are asked to smoke a certain brand of cigarettes and drink a certain whiskey.

After prohibition, the so-called dry regime, could it be that the United States of America is at the point of succumbing to an inundating downpour?

*

* *

If America could stand the truth, it could be revealed that one of her most illustrious children, Lindberg, was her mortal enemy, when, with the feat of a wing in 1927, he linked her to Europe above the head of the Statue of Liberty. There are acts that even a Liberty rooted to the spot can't abide. This exploit was a resounding victory for Americans, but not for the country, very vulnerable from that point on. The plane made the American walls collapse. People were supposed to breathe easily when, after a thousand difficulties, panting, they perceived in the night, like a protecting spirit, the giant Statue of Liberty! At least they were entering another world. The gates of a haven, of an Eden were opening up. Far away, very far, very very far behind them were worries, insults, misunderstandings; ahead—adventure, fortune, honors. They were entering another community, where in order not to disrupt national unity, to maintain team spirit and the hope of success, to promote brotherhood and avoid the stings of pride, demand of each individual his devotion to higher goals, the Americans have of their own free will forbidden the wearing of decorations at receptions. Thus, people go there with their heart and their name, instead of their worldly status. Every American wants to be young. Well, Lady Liberty used to have heart-to-heart talks and console people but now planes fly over her disrespectfully; giant steamers cruise under her nose, forgetting to salute her because such greetings are reserved for buildings in the very powerful United States of America, where daily life goes on between two poles: the Up and the Down, success or failure. Citizens are constantly running toward the Up, the summit, the observation tower. Thousands of well-oiled elevators, unobtrusive and proud of their majestic role, carry their load in a flash up to the thirtieth floor. And the lazy ones inside are helpless without machines and wait for the doors to open automatically. If the doors refused to let them out, the people would beg them, by telephone of course, to condescend to free them. Some of these machines are so tired they're out of breath and can hardly open; they have acquired a soul from carrying hordes of individuals with such diverse dreams.

America is a feverish factory, where new ways of building and living are worked out. Unfettered competition and takeover wars keep everyone awake: it's unlikely that Americans have ever been able to relax. They would not only be overrun by others but overtaken by events. So—they probably live the life of a student the night before an exam and sleep in shifts, trained so that nothing that happens in the world escapes this effervescent state. Americans always have their eyes open, but don't confuse them with those sleepwalkers inhabiting old nations: it isn't unlikely that the hotel doorman, who has been hailing taxis for years, continues blowing his whistle at night, when he is home.

Here is a nation which has perfected colonial methods of exploitation and intends to try them out around her.

Why be surprised to hear Americans described as monsters or a new species invading the continent? What else can they do, these people who are working while the rest of the world is sleeping and dreaming? Happy, rich, powerful people—bosses who complicate existence with restaurants without wine and cafeterias without beer. Paris bears the largest share of responsibility for the strange behavior of these noble citizens. When you give a country such a huge and hollow Liberty as the one blocking the entrance to the so-called new continent, you have to accept responsibility for all the consequences. Carried away by who knows what giddiness of heart or spirit, Paris certainly lacked moderation. And Americans view this Liberty skeptically. What freedom is left for Paris, Europe, the world if such a colossus is given to one country? It's understandable why so many things creak in other parts of the world: they lack liberty. Behaving just like young people ignorant of their history and making no effort to comprehend it, many people talk about dissention between Paris and the city of tall buildings, whereas Paris and New York are the best friends in the world. Paris understands the American taste for Liberty, having given a monument to her as a gift; New York, in its turn, made Paris prosperous by giving a vine stock.[21] Who got the bad end of the bargain? Thus, there are the recurrent arguments and bad blood between these two bewitching capitals, who keep quarreling and making up behind everyone's back, domestic quarrels which could never reach the divorce stage because Paris would not know what to do with Liberty if New York returned it. And neither would New York with the American wine from Bordeaux. The best American ambassador on French soil was that famous vine stock. It's said that Bordeaux, maintaining a warm love for America, has not forgotten it. Wines drunk by American tourists all seem to come from Bordeaux; they're still only drinking wine from home even though abroad. If they happen to look at the label, it's to be convinced that it's from their corner of Bordeaux. This kinship, this mutually beneficial alliance must have given the city its great expansive energy: American yeast makes French bread dough rise.

When eating, Americans most often prefer to drink water or tea to reassure the British lion, suspicious and grumpy in his dotage, that the American eagle would never lay a glove on his interests. Instead at the same time she carries the dazzling Stars and Stripes to the ends of the earth, America extends the zone of influence of her home country: the George Washington Bridge, which crosses the Hudson in one stride, though not a modern Saratoga, does make Mother England proud of her little monsters, and does announce to all the world that America was right to bolt from her British guardians. See how she flaunts her successes, how she demands admiration of her maturity, the muscles of iron, steel, and gold developed since she cut the umbilical cord? Her fabulous riches—just look at her numerous philanthropic millionaire bosses—justify her audacity. In America money must serve man, and it only makes interest by accident since its duty is to work rather than to produce. If it should happen to produce, being extremely fertile, then it's wonderful to see it return with its brood, like a valiant warrior home from some distant battlefield. The old ogre's teeth attributed to this unselfish country do not express reality. Instead, they're the teeth of a

21. The grafting of European varieties such as this Bordeaux vine stock on American rootstocks created European-American hybrids resistant to phylloxera, which had wiped out many vineyards in the late nineteenth century.

baby ogre (America has not stopped growing), making and overseeing thousands of manhole covers, always checking in a magic mirror for the name of her next victim, tolerating no competition. Everyone everywhere is wondering what will become of the world when this ogre grows up? Fortunately, it's taking its time growing up but perhaps just to improve its digestion. The situation seems hopeless for its victims, most of whom panic and present themselves hypnotically on the sacrificial altar. Reading their newspapers, Americans pretend to see nothing. The cries, tears, death rattles? They confuse them with myriad traffic sounds. There is no way the American juggernaut could go by without causing damage and accidents. Those great healers bent over the world's bedstead know it well. Those great generals also understand that an army can't withdraw without having reached the millions of men to be sacrificed to save the honor of automatic weapons, to appease the hunger and thirst of cannons, merely waste products which could impede the progress of the universe and which are simply kicked aside. For centuries men have been thinking this way: would America not lose face if she were suspected of thinking otherwise? if for her also men didn't serve as shield and target for machines spitting out mortality? America has stopped halfway along her journey toward independence. She drags behind her heavy chains, too many people, half-starved or gluttonous hitchhikers that slow her evolution. It's their only way not to miss the boat. The problem is that these people, joined by fate to bring something new to the world, are making the same old mistakes and indulging in a futile racial struggle. Faced with so much hunger, they no longer know what to share. Is that what they're looking for in the pages of their daily newspapers? Do they actually read? Who can verify that Americans finish reading their voluminous newspapers? What else could they do with their weekend?

What can you read while being jostled along on the One Way, where there are no inviting cafés? Just like cars stopping at a service station, people go into cafeterias to fuel up. Could there even be a One Way for dreams and love?

As if draped and showcased in store windows to be admired, American women murmur "Don't touch me." Oh no, Americans do not just read, they speed-read; the sheer bulk of their newspapers scares me. I was almost forgetting that I was in the land of dinosaurs, not dragonflies. Why read when there is the TV, that beneficial timesaving digest. Because of their love of research, Americans, who will travel armed with binoculars and cameras, a throwback to caravan days, race through newspapers in order never to be caught off guard. To greet you, they extend a stiff arm as if to knock you out of their territorial waters. These new citizens are still thin-skinned; fearing competition, they keep you at arm's length.

Although Americans keep their hands hidden under the table while they eat, give them a million dollars and they still won't signal when they're behind the wheel. But they'll freely signal to say pass or go to hell, "One Way, no standing here." Indeed, America is so huge and full of different sights and products that it's difficult to know whether to stop or what to admire, so Americans plunge directly ahead in a quest for new horizons and sensations. They leave honeycomb cells like worker bees buzzing toward a tantalizing flower on magnificent express-ways. An infernal speed race. "No standing here." America going full steam ahead can't sit still. Accustomed to performance, she will die if one day she has to stand still.

*
* *

Men here will do anything to mend fences with Paris! Not only do they make sure to promote French business by drinking wine at meals, but they carry their aggressiveness to the point of saying constantly "le pêché," "le chasse" and "le trouée" which they write "Thruway"[22] to allay suspicion and tame a bit the legendary sensitivity of the Gallic roosters. In the same way, they will gladly say "ya, yes" but never "oui," as if Parisians hadn't also become American. In order to smooth things over—for they're very clever—they drive on the right, blow their horns at night, curse at the wheel, think that women do not understand the rules of the road, and too often dream at the wheel. They have done even more, naming numerous streets La Fayette. Paris, meanwhile, remains skeptical because the crux of the problem stays the same: the American stock brings gold into Parisian cash registers; Parisian liberty brings none into American ones. Point number one!

Paris got rid of its excess of liberty by giving them a statue which is now a burden because it isn't higher than the Empire State Building.

22. Dadié is playing on the idea of agreement. The French say "la chasse" but gender does not always seem to be respected. *La peche* becomes "le pêché," *la chasse,* "le chasse." *La trouée* meaning "opening" becomes "le trouée" (pronounced "thruway"), thus a play on words.

Such a shriveled-up Liberty which does not succeed in innervating all the states is an affront to national honor. Point number two!

Finally, when this Liberty is mentioned, Paris responds with the mischievous smile of one who has made a good deal.

— Oh! don't talk to me anymore about that. You have it—well, keep it!

America, thus, is stuck with her, like an abandoned child, this Liberty made in Paris. Point number three!

Having become an American thing, Liberty can henceforth be exported under a specific brand name. Certain states which accuse America of going the wrong way can't understand this. Having too many cares on their heart and shoulders, Americans work themselves silly in order to forget them; more precisely, they work furiously to "work machines silly." What would they not exploit to keep their superiority? The sun and moon lingering daily to admire the Empire State Building prove that America is the most powerful and modern country in the world, but do not ask for "martini-gin" in just any bar: the term has not gotten a visa to enter the United States of America yet. Try it and a bartender will put ice cubes in your glass. Do not refuse those ice cubes—that would scandalize everyone because ice is necessary for every occasion. How could Americans carry the weight of the world with "hot blood"? Ice freezes a number of human feelings in a world such as ours, where you must stay cool to slice through multiple litigation, disentangle divergent interests, and persevere with established plans against winds and tides. Here, then, food is eaten cold, drinks drunk cold, ice sucked and crunched. As soon as a child is born, parents give him cold milk to drink to make him acquire American cool very early. The big teeth of the baby ogre are frozen, bugbears for unsuspecting nations. Perhaps they can bite more cruelly since they're insensitive; nevertheless, America stays within certain bounds, never sating her appetite in just any circumstance. She owes that to her cold blood. It makes you wonder if this is perhaps America's glacial period, if America is struggling to hasten the coming of the thermal era, if all the progress made is not just a vulgar mask hiding her real goal.

Martini-gin! After having refused the ice, be especially careful to not let anyone see you mixing the martini-gin. The bartender will just throw up his hands and shake his head. For two cents, he will alert the neighborhood. He pities you for not being American and wonders how people can still dally around and not be in the sphere of the great, not make themselves American! People behind the times, people with bizarre tastes could profit from lining up under the star-spangled banner! Who in this life doesn't seem strange to others?

*
* *

These bees emerge on Friday night, buzzing from honeycomb buildings, and flee the city to gather honey from the flowers adorning their beautiful homes tucked away in green belts around New York. These homes come in all shapes and colors, with tarred circular driveways and long ascending staircases. They appear on knolls, on hilltops; some cling to cliffs by a fingertip. There are no barriers between them. Not all strange and selfish customs have crossed the border of the United States of America, still in search of their way. Community spirit's carried so far that sometimes there are no doors on public facilities, where a free circulation of air is certainly useful! But are such open facilities not there to remind tourists that the young nation is still under construction, still growing up and conscious of her deficiencies?

Everyone knows that America ignores fans and screens and lives in the open: she has an athlete's body and displays it shamelessly, like a model. This country is an immense workshop with numerous bosses. Is it surprising that the striptease was born in one of the alleys meandering at the foot of her buildings? This type of court martial for women is yet another test that America gives to other nations. Men who rarely get excited and who docilely stand in line to wait for a bus that will come in an hour can watch striptease shows calmly. Not easily roused, they are a torch rather than a flashlight. Their self-control allows Americans to analyze at one time the attributes of ten or twenty contestants. Operating like an expert, he can also be a magnet but a magnet held at the end of a chain for big projects or important deals. Down from his pedestal, this boss does not always know how to behave: is he harmful? amusing? understanding? Is he in sync? Ahead of the beat? slow on the upbeat? understood? He is all of this, because there is in the American person, the boss, the apostle, the continent, the flag, and the Empire State Building, the world's tallest building. What can be seen clearly, what real contact can be established when he is used to seeing everything either from underground or through the clouds from the fortieth floor?

Conscious of their vitality, weight, and volume, their role as a star, a model, Americans exercise their wits to stay young, whence a taste for study, parades, fanfare, and collective noise—a young people promoted by excessive wealth to the rank of guide of the world, a world of money, where man is struggling to find a niche, a sea of gold smothering and taking thousands of victims in its powerful waves. The gods always need sacrifices: man is the most beautiful object that can be offered. Is he not made in the image of God? Thus, to rivet man to machine and subject him to every degradation is doubtless to dominate the god in him—a patient god, to whom experts preach more patience. Given the fate reserved for him in each individual, he needs it. It's really God being reached through man. What need does he have to come to earth to compete for a salary and distractions? Disloyal competition which would be unpardonable. Perhaps man would be better treated if there were in him no God whose role is to help carry the Golden Empire.

Torn between her role as new torch and her passion to lead her own life, America is searching for equilibrium.

*

* *

You must attend a church service in order to understand to what degree the American is a pilgrim in search of a new Jerusalem. Not knowing whether he will have to decamp tomorrow for another destination, he thanks the Lord passionately. For the moment, parents serve children at meals: they distribute the manna. Through them God gives the daily bread, and so no one eats without having prayed, head bowed. In reaction, Protestants, those specialists in all forms of protest, pray standing up. Their overflowing vitality makes them take extreme positions which sometimes pull the world out of certain quagmires. As in other cases, these are not illnesses requiring surgery but warning bells for life, which does not wish to stagnate in coffers or in fonts. These are people who, having yelled "fire," are taken for arsonists. Are they not the cause of scandal? Thus, Protestant Americans remember the first Spanish-Italian who got down on his knees to pray as soon as he landed on Redskin territory. But he had to die in crass poverty because he didn't know how to get himself noticed. The lords of the earth insist that we kneel before them. But it's not proper to kneel. You have to be tall to be seen, to get noticed. So people will pray to God standing up in order not to confuse Him with nonentities of the earth. Obviously kneeling before both God and a king places them on the same level, associates them, degrades the former while acknowledging the schemes of the latter. This is the eighth deadly sin that had been overlooked, and Protestants emphasize it by their bearing.

To be seen and to be sought after! Is there any wonder that the United States of America worships publicity and public relations? Are we not in a world where it's essential to beat your own drum? Modesty and humility are outmoded. Here, where you must be up to date, one forgets that, for a man, to be born is already to be up to date. Does he intend to take on a new look, to emerge at last from his prisons? Being with it is to have arrived, to have succeeded, to be showcased—ostensibly visible. However, being with it sometimes requires more resources than you have. Then you resort to credit—now the mainspring in the American economy; it sweeps you away and shakes up the world in a powerful vortex that weak constitutions can't resist. From time to time fortunes sink as new peaks surface, to tempt citizens along their winding paths. Credit—a spinning top among the serrations, shelves, gearboxes, reefs—exists to turn the gigantic machine. More industrial and commercial than peasant, Americans take liberties that astonish those attached to the earth, whose civilization has for a long time been integrated with plants and seasons. Wanting freedom from the earth, America is demanding everything from her laboratories and machines. Duped by publicity, citizens become putty in the hands of producers. Under such conditions, how can anyone not forget a bank balance and bounce checks? A simple misdeal in this card game. Credit is the blood that keeps America in feverish motion. Suppress it and America dies of anemia, strangled. The silvering falls off the mirror, revealing great distress underneath; the duchess's makeup disappears, revealing a face refusing to acknowledge its own ugliness. The country realizes this and knows that, contrary to the wisdom of the proverb, money that rolls does gather moss.[23] So America maintains the status quo.

The brouhaha that surrounds celebrities, the constant honking, even at night, comes from the American phobia of being unnoticed. Can anyone escape notice with such brightly lit streets? Americans are deeply contradictory; they want to be just like one of the gang and, at the same time, remain the lionized boss. So there they are, confused, seeking equilibrium for themselves and for the world. Didn't they abscond with the old nations' scale for judging other peoples? Now, those nations are sized up, but by whom? By hyperactive punks, little devils with whom it's always necessary to come to terms, but only

23. The proverb says "a rolling stone gathers no moss."

after much wheedling and flattery. A complex and tragic situation, indeed.

In his never-ending pursuit of a happy day, the American always exhorts, "Have a nice day." Nice for him and for others because he is convinced that his crusade will slowly usher in the day when the whole world will break bread together at a new Last Supper. But America—in whose cities, born of angles and squares, there are no winding streets, no Pasadas, no games of hide-and-seek in the moonlight, nor yet any streets named Good News, Cherry Tree, or Singing Fountain—continues to pulverize men in her fiendish jaws, to wash, dry, and iron them in countless laundries in order to give them that impeccable cachet "made in the United States of America," lanky chic in an embroidered shirt, with the passion for smoking Salem—a sign of peace.[24]

Because of poor publicity, this country, which should have been called Columbia, became America, and the friends of Columbus blame Saint Christopher for such carelessness. Who would not be exhausted after having carried a god on his shoulders? But the greatest paradox is that this region, populated by Redskins called Indians, is the exclusive property of Europeans called Americans. In view of all these internal contradictions, just try to understand something of this immense country, which even white natives do not understand because television only shows fragmentary aspects of it: the head of a president whose legislature has its days numbered, herds of sheep who will go to slaughter the next day, a new rotary press heading for the scrap heap, a superfortress with a great range, only to be outclassed tomorrow by a "hypersuperfortress" with unlimited scope. This is America, which would be killed if her credit were cut off.

Having a weakness for Paris, Americans have not accorded Genoa its rightful place in their heart. Speaking of Genoa, Italy is misunderstood. New billionaire bosses are restoring Versailles, which is also the name of a famous pastry, but Genoa remains snubbed. Yet the Italians, very practical and consummate diplomats, show everyone the ruins of Columbus's house as if to say: "Look what adventure gets you! Would his home be destroyed today if he had not placed himself in the service of those other Spanish slavers? Where is the famous American generosity when it leaves in ruins the house of the man who discovered the

24. Dadié may be referring to the publicity of that era, which emphasized the springtime, air-softened, thus peaceful, taste of Salem cigarettes, as well as to the fact that "salem" means "peace" in Hebrew.

New World? How can you have confidence in this country which has had no regard for Christopher Columbus's home?" And they point out the ivy, the half-ruined stones. A man who loved sciences and adventure lived there, a man who gave a homeland to other men and allowed them to create a new way of life.

Is there not in New York a statue of the famous navigator at Columbus Circle? Is it the American people's fault if the surrounding buildings didn't have the sensitivity to respect this illustrious man, if they crush him under all their concrete weight. To crush Columbus is to badly misunderstand the man, who triumphed over the anger of the elements and of his crews. To be Spanish-Italian is to combine virtues and faults, to have wide shoulders and the strength of a bullfighter in order to contain the bellicose encroachment of buildings. But who can tell whether tomorrow this man, who stubbornly refuses to grow by an inch under the most favorable rains and winds, will not be considered too short?

In view of these cursory observations, the feverish urge for movement that animates the American is understandable, also why the George Washington Bridge spans the Hudson, why the Lincoln Tunnel goes under the Hudson, and the Brooklyn Cattery Tunnel under the East River. America learned from history in order to barricade herself in her way of life.

To curb the destructive instincts of those who, like Fernando de Soto, would return from Europe with crosses and dogs trained to chase Indians—a sport now out-of-date—the first Americans had the fortunate idea of naming their capital Philadelphia, which was quite an agenda. "But where are the snows of yesteryear"[25] when iron teeth crush men and continents, and when police dogs jump down the throats of other citizens? Fernando de Sotos no longer come from a Europe with loose teeth, demanding news in return, but from a wrought-up America, some of whose citizens have a retina that is very sensitive to the color black. Anchored in the time of the slave trade, American ships no longer seem to know which horizon to steer for. In this, the country does not seem to have left the European groove. Are we to conclude that if the black had been a descendant of Cain, he would have had a right to more consideration in relations with other peoples? What a strange crime to see a father's nakedness! It's acknowledged that Noah

25. In the poem by François Villon, "Ballade des dames du temps jadis," the famous line in French is "Mais où sont les neiges d'antan?" Dadié is suggesting there is no need for nostalgia in remembering these events.

was not black, and we end up wondering how Ham[26] himself could produce people of another color if the devil was not mixed up in it! This thorny problem annoys many Americans, so they keep colleagues at a distance, like contagious cases they're carefully studying.

America has not succeeded in bridging the gap between various colors. She has tamed rivers, but not subtleties. Who would dare run the risk of being weaned in order to tell the truth? What courtier would play the court jester and die of hunger? All her sucklings know they will never be allowed to grow up. Is her milk too cold, too synthetic? An excessively watchful mother who shoves you under her with often brutal beak and foot blows when danger menaces, she only allows chaperoned outings, freedom without rupture; like European powers, she dons a new mask and prolongs the carnival.

This boss thinks he will never have enough land to build his buildings, enough tracks for the dollar chase, enough people to admire his artificial flowers. Wheeler-dealer and pioneer, he sees the entire world as an arena ripe for his experiments, so do not mention to him the immense feelers he puts out: he will look at you as if you are crazy because he represents the most democratic people in the world. In a certain sense this is true, considering the attitude of certain satellite states. Could the powerful American shadow stop growing and evolving? When you see the pleasant country homes, you know why the United States of America is pushing its borders so far out—to roll tranquilly for days amid greenery, birds and streams. Americans are dreamers who get brutal when rudely awakened. Therefore they're sometimes extremely inquisitive, especially when they see red. Just as with bulls, red exasperates and excites them. Could they also be aware of the dangers in the stirrings of other peoples? Do they think whites have been a threat to entire tribes? Has the danger been averted? Who would dare ask America the question? The huge expansive force of America, now a measuring rod for everyone, has its roots in the hunger and thirst of others.

Parisian gourmets will turn up their nose at boiled meat, salad without salt, vinegar, or pepper. Who would think of these trifling ingredients when thinking of dropping anchor the next minute for who

26. Ham in the Bible is Noah's second son, the father of Canaan and the peoples of southern Arabia, Ethiopia, and Egypt. Ham's disrespect for Noah earned Canaan a curse. Cain, the first son of Adam and Eve, later killed his brother Abel because of jealousy. Punished, he was condemned to a life of wandering, marked to warn attackers that he was under God's protection.

knows what destination? In this long peregrination, Americans have reached the Pacific, swum in its waters, drunk from them. How can anyone gazing at himself and swimming in the Pacific be accused of a warlike spirit?

Peace has become the balloon the great nations of this world play with, while fearful peoples bring down the house as if to mute their own whisperings. The river beds of the franc and the dollar may be full of dangerous alligators, but the countries that know the pathways, that have taken root at the foot of a tree, near the water, and have tasted of the new apple, are slowly in the process of changing their appearance under the magic wand of the fairy, America. They, in their turn, have discovered they're naked and are trying to stay warm beside the great powers of the world.

*
* *

In folktales, animals dress up like men, wearing hats, pants, shirts, or jackets. Men civilize the animals of the bush by indoctrinating them with their habits and customs. Snow White, Cinderella, Peter Pan, Dumbo, and Tar Baby supply stories handed down through the centuries. Tar Baby was made from a block of tar softened by Brer Fox to fool Brer Rabbit, who was trapped because he tried to box Tar Baby.

To imagine Harlem in Manhattan and that Tar Baby could be a block of softened tar illustrates total and absurd blindness. How can you say that the black chauffeur, the black maid, the famous black singer—all part of the national pride and joy—come from a block of softened tar? People talk about America and the black problem but they can't find a solution. Well, the solution is this. Blacks are the tar used to cover roads and so we are all loaded with guilt for rolling over them! We can now understand the meaning of brakes screeching to a halt on the roads. Sometimes it's a prayer, sometimes a curse, at other times a song. Blacks play their role even on the highways, making life pleasant for others. But when they lift their head, drivers lose theirs. And so people talk about a mysterious accident since everything was going so well. They had forgotten the tar-covered blacks, had not taken them into account.

*
* *

Remembering tales of fabulous prehistoric beasts—dinosaurs, tyrannosaurs, Americans dream of becoming something fabulous for the present, of leaving a lasting impression on history. When future excavators, looking for lost civilizations, reach the American skeletons, the whole world will explode with the joy of finally rediscovering the new Atlas who, during the gloomy twentieth century—in the era when man was searching for his own worth—carried on his phenomenal shoulders the fate of the so-called free world, a world where freedom of commerce was in mortal combat with human freedom. Perhaps there might then be no more barriers and colors; no one would lead the life of wandering beasts, jumping from valley to valley, continent to continent, pursued by hunger and persecuted because of their ideas; having finally emerged from his cocoon, man would be a magnificent butterfly. However, playing the titan while standing only a few inches high is very amusing for spectators observing this country shouting herself breathless in her proud climb. How long will the spectacle go on? Barely able to keep up with their country's feats, many Americans also wonder.

Filling America with Empire State Buildings is not a frightening job for these twentieth-century Cyclopes. One eye! One Way! a natural combo! When developers gaze up at the top floor of a project, they're thinking about the ideal form their continent must be, admiring with a keen eye her big lead over the rest of the world, and dreaming about the next cloud to be dispersed for more living space. Buildings with such solid foundations give free rein to the wildest dreams. By preventing traffic jams in streets and minds, the One Way fosters the realization of fantastic projects buzzing around in American heads. Since America is a laboratory staffed by researchers and specialists, it's understandable that certain types of persons become guinea pigs and just as logical that even these poor bastards would never agree to give up their status, always first class. The American nationality is the only one you do not renounce; rarely do Americans turn into Europeans or Africans. It's easy to develop a taste for the slick American track, which allows no time to realize that at every turn some flunky is demanding a pound of flesh. It's up to each individual to make quicker turns in order to escape the invisible hands reaching out at each corner. Here in America, where people seem to exist to allow others to be happy, the right to live is costly. Americans are inexhaustible treasure troves, exceptionally fertile soil, new strains carefully cultivated for high productivity, in other words, infinitely capable of absorbing more and more.

The question "Is the American really a Cyclops?" is debatable. Does he think he can shear all the sheep in the world, then feed and clothe them identically? Will he succeed where so many others have failed? If everyone marches along to the same drummer, then masters will no longer be masters! But how beautiful and smart the marionette show seems from the rarefied height of wheeling and dealing, a very exciting circus led by an ironfisted tamer who knows when to give them cake.[27] He blatantly rots the teeth of his flock so they will be ashamed to open their mouths. The measuring unit: the foot. When all America reaches the height of the Empire State Building, prayers sent on high from synagogues, mosques, churches, and temples will only have to follow the same path, the One Way, giving luster to the beautiful star taken by the new gods from Broadway in order to play John the Baptist and prepare the way for the future coming of the Son of God.

The bosses and tycoons of Wall Street are impatiently awaiting the second coming in order to show Jesus how they have fattened up his donkey and installed him next to the Golden Calf, how his thirty denarii have continued to multiply. Certain New Testament parables had not fallen on deaf ears after all. Times have greatly changed. Christ's renown has become universal. And America, a very understanding and vigilant guardian of His doctrine, which she applies in very practical ways, will value Him even more, in billions of dollars. Knowing Americans very well, Jesus hesitates; but He is patient and watchful and won't be caught unprepared. His sense of smell does not fail Him. Some nose! Let us talk a bit about this "tactile" organ, which, on certain billionaires, is so huge. But don't expect to find these lucky noses, these genial noses in the streets. Those who have them would remove them to disguise themselves before leaving home. So you can jostle Americans, but please don't touch their nose. How can you tell the false from the true? Simple, once you think of it. As simple as the difference between an egg and Christopher Columbus. The man who has a natural nose can blow his nose without turning his head. What does he have to hide? So, since many Americans turn their head to blow their nose... At last, let us take a break, leaving the nose-tunnel in order to reach the heights of Times Square, the world's liveliest crossroads, Harlem, the world's largest black city, Macy's, the world's largest department store, the Tappan Zee Bridge, the world's longest and most modern—all famous monuments to the exceptional American vitality.

27. A possible allusion to Marie Antoinette's dismissal of the people, "let them eat cake."

There are, of course, gloomy shadows at the foot of these masterpieces, but what other country could have run so smoothly and so fast, if it had had at its baptismal fonts those same strange sponsors from Rome, Paris, Amsterdam, London, and if it had not ceased to attract and charm them by its youthful beauty? And America has placed them in communities, in fraternities to more easily digest them. While waiting for that ultimate time, she offers them her magnificent highways to stir them up, to deafen them, to dazzle them with speed so that they will get rid of the traces that could prevent them from being worthy children of the United States of America.

America, with its facade of buildings, doesn't know how to smile. She increases opportunities only to withhold them. Stores only know how to snicker at neighboring stores, always trying to outwit them. Even with all the luxury, their vast aisles, persuasive salespersons, casualness, and openness, there is no poetry! There is no heart, even on the job. People working to earn a living, their right to existence, can't wait to hear that it's break time. Everything here in America seems mobilized for an unconditional win; every person unwittingly becomes an enemy to conquer and pillage. America throws a harsh light on both the strengths and weaknesses of Western civilization, which uses men as fodder for voracious machines and cannons. It's quite possible, as seen here, to build up without evolving, without giving man his full value, without resolving a thousand and one pressing problems. As a problem solver, America has aged prematurely and seems to run in circles around her buildings like a caged lion. She seems suspended, silhouetted against a utopia which she will never reach and earth, from which she has blindly wrenched herself. Nothing more than a citadel for businessmen! A battlefield for Homeric struggles! Even a spectacular death causes no stir; even suicides from the numerous bridges of New York and elsewhere are rare. Woe to the weak of constitution in America!

Tall buildings cause cricks in the neck; the shrill publicity is depressing. Everything seems excessive. It's useless to get Americans together in offices, mix them in cafeterias or the subway; they remain strangers, each one tenaciously pursuing his own dreams, each one stubbornly trying to make it. People seem like organization men, united by a universal work ethic. Organization men first and foremost, Americans second, as an afterthought. They remember to be American only when they catch sight of a flag displayed in some corner.

Having succeeded brilliantly, the little American terror juggles the heads, hearts, and consciences of states and continents. He wants to be the maestro of a world symphony. He is prepared to construct buildings of six hundred, a thousand, ten thousand stories to house the entire world, to self-destruct even in order to realize his dearest dream—that every person, spoon-fed, get in step with America. Was he not playing with rockets while others were tangled up in kite strings? Was he not the first to experiment with the terrifying power of the bomb?

*
* *

The excitement sweeping over men is so intense that firemen are constantly on their feet and worn out: for them, the country is a giant smoldering volcano.

Let Paris try to add a centimeter to her famous Eiffel Tower and the Empire State Building will also grow by several hundred inches, for competition over ridiculous things has spread to the entire world. Everyone has lost sight of man, the basic element in the struggle. One has succeeded in pitting him against himself in a passion for appearances, which causes him to miss living. Even with simple customs, can anyone ever get to the heart of the matter if they're caught in multiple nets? Everyone, everyday is becoming a mummy whose heart, restrained by a parade of psalms, sometimes jerks awake to wonder if faith is not threatened in some disreputable corner of the world. God doesn't demand that golden temples be built but that the brothers of Jesus Christ be cared for. Time must do its work; the ages must unfold. The world is only several billions of years old and man has barely left the ape stage. What would it cost God to end misfortunes if they offended Him?

Saint Peter's in Rome is only a fake. The real Saint Peter's is in America—a fact many people don't know. To obtain grace from heaven and earth, the initiated go to the street of the Wall of Supplications and Bleeding[28] in the New Bethlehem, where they're required to smoke Salem—to make peace. Obviously in a seething period of cold war, a smoked peace is easier to preserve. There had to be America to dream

28. An allusion to the Wall of Lamentations in Jerusalem. Dadié refers to America as the world's creditor, for whom beggars must obey many rules and regulations in order to obtain mercy.

that up. A smoked peace is ready to be canned and the United States of America is preparing, tomorrow, to send tons of peace to the entire world. Who knows, we might also have filets, minced meat, and marmalade of peace to accompany the caviar at cocktail hour.

*
* *

Americans are right to be angry at Paris for having given them such a colossal liberty, a monster at the entrance of the city, frightening everyone. Even her most ardent lovers are appalled at sight of her. Three meters from one ear to the other. A mastodon, a prehistoric liberty. All of America could enter her and still not fill her up. And for individuals used to thinking in inches and feet, it's impossible to measure the dimensions, the weight, and value of this Liberty that Europe consistently devalues every five years. The United States of America forgets that Paris has confidence in her to protect Western freedom, constantly threatened with submersion by some new hysterical outbreak. Who could have lifted or played with this liberty if she were full? And who would have agreed to cast a full liberty? What artistic genius would have made such a glaring error?

This Liberty has become embarrassing, just like a whitlow, ever since factories began to spew their not-yet-finished products onto other continents. How can new territory be obtained without bumping into liberty a bit? How can people be contained without bruising them? Fortunately, there's the American nose, a gold mine of inexhaustible resources allowing its owner to sniff out, encircle, and master all traps, making him so astute that Americans, who, people think, are easily embarrassed, embarrass others by their ability to get out of wasp's nests. They leave Liberty on an island, for them the sign of an era. Understanding the twists and turns of the Parisian heart, Wall Street observes her skeptically. The volume of the gift especially does not appeal to him in the least. Nonetheless, is that sufficient reason for Liberty to remain unproductive in a country killing herself to accumulate all the gold in the world? And there she is—sold on stamps sent to the whole world, a re-export according to the rule book. America sells freedom, just as women sell flowers, with a calm smile and a clear conscience.

— Do you want some flowers?
— Do you want some peace?

— Say it with flowers.
— Say it with freedom.

It's clear now that freedom risks becoming just another American product—synthetic, artificial. Powdered freedom? Who wants some? Soluble freedom, instant mix!!!

On the other hand, anything this nation cannot bring herself to do, she entrusts to her enemies the Japanese, who, back home now, no longer dream of conquering the world. So it is that tourists buy bronze replicas of this gigantic Liberty as they tour Manhattan on Circle Line boats. An adaptation of Liberty, scaled down into inches, feet—liberties you can pocket as a souvenir, sensitive liberties that have to be watched constantly like fragile flames. Thus, America diminishes freedom, but by means of the Asians, who haven't yet caught on.

After such a feat, there's is no way to pass Americans off as naive angels! They're even now eyeing the chance to palm off on Europe the remains of this huge Liberty. If they stand guard on the Rhine, it's only to find a future site for this phenomenal freedom, trampled by tourists who line up not to reflect, meditate, or dream, but only to view the city and the sea. For Liberty to become a mere promontory is a defeat, all the more resounding and humiliating in America, where the abnormal is the norm. Some Americans suffer because of the downfall of freedom on their continent, seeing freedom trampled in the land of liberty; but what can they do when enemies flock in from all over the world, even Paris, to climb the shoulders of this memorable statue, not to feel her strength or admire the flame that lifts the gloom but to look at the skyline. Is it America's fault if people have perverted taste and can no longer understand anything about symbols? America always thought that tourists, after several hours within the body of freedom, would come out with a more precise conception of what she stands for, a more ardent love. Alas, they almost all leave with building plans in their head and pockets, projected treaties in their briefcases, and the will to become Americans in their own country. Then why continue to maintain Liberty if others no longer recognize her value, if they delude themselves with iron and cement, artificial flowers and Broadway lights? And so, every day America is more and more convinced of the superiority of her technological civilization. Why not? When you climb up to the crown of Liberty, when you cling to her torch to admire the Empire State lights, visible from three hundred miles, you have the proof that

America can lead the world in the future. She feels it her imperial duty to save peace and freedom from every attempted sacrilege. She watches her supergiant bombers and her thousands of soldiers ready to pounce on all fronts so that factories, thrown into endless competition, can keep on running. Produce, produce! the password. Competition with other nations is all economic. Who will blanket the world with her products, her flag, her ideas, and mannerisms? Who will be the boss, the tutor for other peoples? Beyond this guardianship, what place will man occupy in society? This problem, which we had solved for ourselves, is here a real predicament, one that robs citizens of sleep. Thus they're on guard, some nursing their poverty, others their fortune, a very democratic society giving everyone a normal place in every branch of activity. An education based on the development of individual desires and the struggle for life has marked every institution with a special personality.

Being American requires a certain courage. You have to get rid of some reflexes and acquire others, just like soldiers in boot camp. As for blacks, for centuries they've stayed in their galleys, in boot camp. They're only put in uniforms that are out-of-date; they're given only rooms that no longer seem habitable. Not just relief troops, they're on an endless journey with all the risks in place. Blacks didn't understand that with emancipation, they were supposed to find a haven, disembark, and then clear the premises. What can they expect in these cold regions that are deadly for them? Barely tolerated, they remain black water, a thick water that was useful for washing cotton and gold but proved unfit for uranium. Despite all the alloys, the dexterity, and profound knowledge of goldsmiths, their features are preserved intact; unassimilatable products. Only their hair seems liable to evolutionary law. These men standing on America's shores, near their boats capsized on numerous reefs, never stop yelling in the showplaces of Harlem, demanding who knows what any longer. Harlem is the refuge of workers on break, the shipwrecked, the disinherited, orphans mistreated by stepmothers—the refuge of men to be integrated but now trapped in jazz as if in an iron corset. Every night Harlem blows the trumpet of Jericho at the feet of Wall Street. Harlem, the funeral home of America, where the tears of blacks are taken to be cries of joy. Harlem daily smothers its sores and boils, its pains, under the frenetic dance steps of its artists: twist, bebop—magical dances done to wear down the unbelievers, prayers addressed to distant gods. Harlem is the black reject who keeps on thumbing his nose at the white world, refusing to be a by-product; jazz in his hands has become fighting music. Rocked to their foundation, walls will someday fall to free him, to finally liberate him from all that jazz. Amplified by microphones, his voice carries so far that buildings have to add floors on top and improve their soundproofing! Blacks obstinately scream away, sure of mastering the elements and dominating negative currents. What would America become if they suddenly stopped singing? A cemetery of driving rods, of feet and inches,[29] because, wonder of wonders, white singers have black accents. Harlem is the poor cousin who sings and dances for his supper and clothes. A philosopher, his songs are proverbs whose deeper meaning is often missed. Unfortunately, black humor still escapes some people.

No doubt Harlem's tunes help keep machines running in that unbridled competition which America delivers to the world. Not having the good fortune to sniff the fragrance of freedom when it passed by, Harlem became the country's minstrel, singing outside castles whose drawbridges remain closed, with a voice as powerful and as charming as the devil's.

Exotic Harlem prospers amidst its garbage—a picturesque complement to the opulence of neighboring areas.

Isolated, quarantined, listed among historical monuments and tourist sights, sold as statuettes on postcards and stamps, Liberty shouldn't be evoked constantly to support causes. To respect man is doubtless neither to limit him nor keep him in poverty. Different economic ideas are fighting it out; ways of judging man are in confrontation. The idea of God is the salad embellishing the main dish: only those who are naive eat it. Anyway, what is this god who has such harsh rancor, such deep-rooted hatred for his own creatures, his own image? A god who underestimates himself in man can only be a second-rate god, a god for businessmen, a continental god; and the color white wasn't given to him accidentally. The white god hasn't yet gone beyond the level of business. But who can be sure that the people here have a god, even when they talk about a white god?

Being American is, first, donning a uniform made in the U.S.A., then assuming habits and attitudes that distinguish a good American, then speaking American because that is thinking American, and thinking American is not to miss a single opportunity to assert the presence of this powerful nation. It's important for people to know that American

29. A play on the word *pouce,* which can mean both thumb and inch.

differs from English: it's not a degenerate dialect.[30] That's why Americans talk and talk, whether you understand them or not. The essential fact is that they have spoken and that you have grasped their meaning. They have spoken American; it's up to you to make an effort to understand them. They have been in the forefront for so long! Look at the docks, wharves, bridges, tunnels, mountain chains they've forced out of the earth; look at their prowess. Don't they also have their obelisk, the most glaring symbol of grandeur? Haven't they taken something from Africa, the land of charms? Is this not a pact linking the two continents? Is America's black population not the living bridge which can unite her to the old African land? Her intentions and her actions, badly misunderstood and distorted by adversaries committed to her defeat, give her a false image. And yet, this land of liberty really wants to be a refuge for everyone. The whole country strives for this goal with a titanic effort, man as much as machine. Pick up the telephone receiver and dial the number: the machine ponders at least two minutes before relaying your order: it can be overheard rummaging through memory and papers. Clearly blunders must not be made among so many communities, fraternities, companies.

Speaking American produces shocking results, immediately placing a foreigner on the American wavelength. He becomes a link in the assembly line, which influences the way every American lives. Up to now the chain was missing as a zodiac sign, but America will have to have it included and adopted peacefully since it's essential to the existence of modern man, trained to live in a gearbox, linked one to another as much by hands as by feet. The chain leading from the machine's mind to man's will replace the Libran scales and be the natural ally of Aries, Scorpio, and Mars, the "maybe" of the Lion and the "perhaps" of Capricorn. As a result of playing the role of minor divinity, the American has such an intimate knowledge of the immense power of the real God that he doesn't bother to show Him either at crossroads to watch over travelers or on rooftops to calm storms. Instead, secular Americans are said to carry Him in their hearts, near the white god enshrined in wallets, a take-charge, pushy god who could very well appear one day in Africa, when America's problems no longer suffice and when her wallets begin to cramp his growing bulk. This image will soon be displayed in museums, where tourists will troop to view the cannibalistic white god in the same way they visit the Empire

30. Dadié uses the term "gui", a plant.

State Building, Notre-Dame, or Saint Peter's. The people of this continent lack a real god. Do they think they'll find him in the jumble of machines which, when returning your change, issue a little ticket saying "Thank-you, call again." Obviously, they have not yet learned to write "Come back." Call again, because everything here can be accomplished by phone. Americans live by the telephone. A person can hole up in a room a hundred years thanks to the telephone. Machines know full well that a customer won't come back in person. What human could repeat "Thank you, call again" all day long to thousands of customers? The machine is a slave that has acquired the American mentality. It too has become civilized—a parrot, a robot.

When Parisians hear the Latin Quarter mentioned, don't let them get carried away singing the praises of America's appreciation of French art and literature. Here the Latin Quarter is a night club! That is what has become of the Latin Quarter, the mecca of French thought—the Sorbonne, the Bibliothèque Sainte-Geneviève, the Collège de France, the Panthéon—since it passed the island of Liberty for Manhattan. It means joy, pleasure, lightheartedness, wit, dance, the exact image of Paris, where attention is "given" whereas in New York attention is "paid." Paris tends to soften angles, takes care to think of others' thirst...

New York, on the other hand requires personal effort by everyone. One of the qualities of this country's citizens is to like clear-cut situations or to pull strings so they become clear-cut, at the very least for themselves, if disconcerting for others. Thus, the varying opinions of America, depending on whether you're at the top or the bottom of the social ladder.

Latin Quarter!—the term doubtless implies respect for the Parisian life-style, for that Paris where Americans feel their hearts break free of the Puritan bonds preventing them from marching to the beat of their own drum—those old bonds that some would like to place on the heart of volcanic Africa to give her a taste for suicide rather than life. Africa—chest open to the wind, bare feet touching the ground, man solidly planted on the earth in order to better look at the sky. But now she is setting off for the present, cloistered, decorated with old ideas, mummified. Old trading post, the signs not yet dim, she aims to become a prison for the African man, the new man with the iron mask of contemporary history.

Latin Quarter! "le pêché," "le chasse," another sign that this language is so fluid it can adapt to others when it goes overseas. And

Parisians, in order to become American, are condemned to say: "le thruway," fists and teeth clenched. But what can be done? It's one of the conditions imposed on anyone who wishes to become a citizen of the United States of America.

But, meanwhile, is there anyone who hasn't heard of the famous Cartesian logic which every Parisian drags around in his baggage, the woman with her lipstick, the man with his toilet kit? Every minute, the woman puts some logic on her lips, and the man, morning and evening, on his cheeks. A bad habit that keeps them from seeing New York with normal eyes. Everything makes them dizzy; therefore one morning, double-quick, they catch the fastest "jet," and yell to all the rooftops below that New York is a country of Redskins with white mentality. No! New York is populated by whites whose mentality is being formed slowly in those cells of buildings; a horde of people stamping their feet impatiently, looking for the way in the tunnel-like streets. The Statue of Liberty, the Empire State Building, and a forest of skyscrapers are the only realities American can still claim.

New York symbolizes the challenge presented to the stodgy Old World by the upstart technological age, the triumph of adventure and risk, the apotheosis of those hungry and thirsty dreamers whose fierce determination attracted groups from the far-flung corners of the earth to a haven, a new home. But what has become of all their grandiose dreams? Buildings have grown so they require men to support them: they get ever higher and higher in order to flash company names all the way to the Indian Ocean. Wall Street maintains narrow back streets to keep certain deals hush-hush. The semi-obscurity favors meditation, the first intimations of altruistic feelings; with no eye contact, it's possible to keep the cool head needed to manipulate gold, the reflection of the white god who thrives on the reverential silence and total humility of his suppliants from whom his minions extract earnest money before granting an audience. A god who must play hard to get is not easy! A mating ritual must be observed, conforming to his habits and customs. Every month you must make offerings called "interest," proof of your orthodoxy. Since ten, fifteen eggs are sometimes required, it seems you must already have a well-provisioned henhouse to knock at the doors of the greedy gods of this continent. I understand why New York chickens have no taste; they're dead-tired from producing eggs for gods that kill by strangling to avoid bloody hands. Very civilized, very powerful, very demanding gods who have eyes and ears and a cult all over the world, whose orders America executes to the letter when she strolls all around the world armed to the teeth. Such unsupportive gods, who hardly reassure America, prevent her from fulfilling her great potential; she failed—being content only to ape, rearrange, amplify. Except for buildings, highways, and bridges, what inspires man in America? She is a shadow transported from a Europe she can't shake. Yet Europe snubs her grotesque caricature, refusing to recognize the monster she bore. And yet the United States of America is only a second Europe, afforded a new scheme of things by the luxury of distance. To join Bismark and Des Moines, St. Petersburg and Rome, Paris and Memphis is no easy task, but didn't Europe start it? Didn't she long to hatch this weird brood? America's vision is even grander: in the amalgam of peoples she stamps with approval, she reserves a gold star for Europe, so she can't be accused of ingratitude!

In Greenwich Village, young people play chess and watch westerns. Is this their silent protest against the assembly line, the One Way, the sounds and flashy publicity of Times Square and the theaters?

Paris still has come clout; just look at the café "Le Figaro."[31] When intellectuals meet under the Beaumarchais hat, near the Renaissance Café and make Figaro say what they dare not say openly, that's a sign that a system is moving toward its goal. Do Americans want off the One Way?—Afro-Americans too? Could the heat of the cafés be starting to melt the ice? Would the white world finally open the sluices of the floodgates to the black flood? That, at last, would sound the death knell of jazz, that din Harlem makes to keep New York charged up, a tropical war dance that entrances everyone, dismal cries by those assassinated on street corners, piercing the New York night. Who hears them anyway, who peeps through the shutters or opens the latch? Who goes out? Who lends a hand to these shipwrecks on the surf-tossed American reef? Who hears the desperate pleas of these women, children, and old people threatened by greedy white foam. In the morning they receive their mouthful of bread so they will cough up the change washed up the day before. Harlem—new raft of Medusa on the Mississippi, the Hudson, or the East River. Harlem—sweat, hunger, tears, laughter—enough to fool the kids. Harlem—church to keep up hopes and cafés to stave off hunger... ! Harlem jazz—the jazz of protest and resistance. Harlem artists—heralds of all those lost in oceans of cotton and tobacco. Harlem daughters—girls watching over strong

31. Figaro is the hero of Beaumarchais's *Le Barbier de Séville* and *Le Mariage de Figaro*.

workers in an immense rice plantation in the lower depths full of music. Harlem—stark neighborhood, "darkwater," backwater in the shadow of tall buildings! Harlem turns on its lights earlier than other neighborhoods to be able to see clearly and dress its wounds. Harlem—the hold of the immense American ship, whose mast is the Empire State Building! Those heartrending cries rising from this African village in the heart of New York—when will they cease?

*

* *

Confusing the glimmers of the red star with the colors of dawn, America is overrun by scarlet ideas. As if Bolshevik vodka and Soviet bread were not enough, the people are applauding the "Russian ballet": the drink, the bread, the steps of "dangerous" dancers have captured the continent of old trappers. America insists on laminating, transforming, and exorcising these three essential elements of life before sending them home to soften Soviet customs. She wants to make them her acolytes. Under the only victory arch in the city (a sign of America's peaceful mood), George Washington is smiling to see people following the lead of their heart and curiosity: American freedom comes across as the freedom of individual equilibrium. Every person can drink what he wants provided he keeps enough blood flowing to the brain to see a red light, and he can eat all the candy he wants, provided he can find a suit to fit. In America's environment of total freedom, it's so easy to lose your head or break down that, as a result, even a rubber check is not a venial sin, only a simple error in math. What in Paris is a crime with serious consequences is in New York a mere trifle. Saint Peter will wear quite a glum expression on his face when he has to open his doors to both Parisian and New York perpetrators, the former sporting ball and chain and the latter a floral halo. Oh yes, the New York criminal will make out just fine, because money in America is so taken for granted that those who play tricks with it or reap rewards have to go to Paris to find the Golden Calf, Greed, and Avarice, and all their inhuman and paralyzing consequences. The proof? Just look at that Parisian at Saint Peter's gate: he is in handcuffs for stealing a paltry sum. It's obvious that Paris does not allow such blasphemy of His Lordship Gold. Once sacred, always sacred, especially such an energetic divinity. To attract gold its worshippers everywhere must honor it. Thus out of respect they use checks as graven images, in order to carry their god everywhere.

It pleases Gold to appear in checkbooks taken from the tailored pockets of the powerful of the earth. The new savior leaves dusty traces from his sandals in all towns and villages after he teams up with small-time merchants to stir up fervor and recruit disciples.

Favorite offspring of gold, the dollar is so prolific that an American takes a thousand and one maddening precautions before returning your change. First, he stares as he sizes you up, then he carefully pulls out a wad of dollars from which he violently jerks each bill by the ear. A dialogue ensues in which the greenback murmurs, then groans, and finally begs before being offered to you. The explanation for the delay: "To see if he was alone." You see, his owner must not slip up and return a female bill. She might reproduce in your cozy pocket. Just to try your patience, the really astute American will even say he has never seen in all his life as an immigration agent such a passport as yours. He can't even lie diplomatically. To what school should he be sent? In what slot would some institution put an American who agreed to attend? Who would agree to be ruined in order to be in charge of him? Has he not become a serious problem for the whole world, a textbook case scrupulously examined by timid researchers who dare not offer any conclusive opinion? After all, who would wantonly ask to be weaned and thus provoke the new Jupiter to rage. Who willingly bites the hand that feeds? Who gets halfway across the river, then insults the local alligator? Naturally, one and all discuss America in hushed tones, savvy about the big stick she wields ...

The drugstore is the concrete expression of the notion of freedom that blooms in America: disease and cure placed side by side. Eat everything you want and buy the remedy you need, a disinfectant or a favorite perfume. America has calculated what all the wasted efforts of man since creation could have produced and now offers the opportunity to be efficient while putting him in bondage. In the drugstore he becomes a link in the assembly line of consumers, just like everywhere else in America, which has had the good fortune not to know feudal presidents and kings. This nation, which would like to be the world's central hub and does everything to get there, lacks that stirring experience.

In New York any person who can't find the store he's looking for needs to have his eyes examined: the huge letters, intense flashiness, diverse colors, multiple movements, rhythmic breathing and neon signs, all in unison, do not just catch your eyes, they literally put them out. Doubtless it's on these premises that some accuse Americans of not always seeing very clearly in world affairs. These diverse and trickling lights are so upsetting and blinding that stunned factories produce the same articles for everyone. Lurid signs all over the world testify to the keen rivalry among firms to capture consumer attention. We grasp the significance of Jesus' error when He chased the merchants from the temple since the whole earth is a temple for business dealers. Even in churches, for the sake of publicity, pictures of heavenly greats are sold. It remains to be seen whether Jesus will oppose His personal propaganda. Besides everyone is awaiting His imminent return. No one knows what colors He will be bearing. For the moment, it doesn't matter since His photos are available, the least of all evils. Meanwhile, the earth continues dutifully making everything bear fruit.

American consumers are treated like the blind, just numbers in this gigantic country of draftees and volunteers, veterans and conquistadors. Consumers give their size, head and chest dimensions, and a package appears. They don't always have time to choose, and what would they choose? They would always see themselves coming and going. Are factories not uniting people by dressing them in the same style? To choose is to waste time, so choice is not yet an American custom. But America has taken a little something from many other cultures: the Latin Quarter from the Parisians, the beehive mentality from the Germans, composure from the British, a taste for music and dance from blacks. The borrowing even goes dangerously far. Didn't I see a store sign saying People's Flowers? It must have been stolen from the Russians. Here in America, mobilized for the survival of great business dynasties, the conquest of markets, and conformity, it's strange to hear talk of offering people flowers to improve taste, which is immediately perverted by mass production in factories exhausted but gloating over their efforts to dress and feed all the Americans who are enmeshed and manipulated at will in their system!... On this fast track, who'll stop first, man or machine? Who knows? They seem to live symbiotically. Just make the least gesture of hand or foot and immediately a taxi stops, a corner of a stamp peeks out, a fast-food window serves you, a Coke pours out, an ice cream cone licks your tongue. An invisible magnet attracts man to machine, drawing the latter inexorably into daily life. All that is left is to put information booths at intersections so the tourist can find the way automatically. This new invention, like a talking clock, would not only make a visitor autonomous, it would make the people of New York City the most independent, the most isolated in the world. Machines would serve them punctually and efficiently. For rarely will an elevator fake sickness, or the telephone be overstressed, or water tire of running, or a calculator have a migraine or dizziness. The charm of America—I had to leave it to fully grasp it—is that her machines are strangely subdued: they seem aware of their assigned role. Conceived and born in a certain environment, American machines do not like to leave home and be handled by foreigners who do not speak their language with the proper accent. They know their worth, the number of stars backing them up.

Every American, insured for life, has become a piece of merchandise, a product. Death has become profitable. In the democratic tradition, it's up to each individual to overestimate or undervalue himself. Nothing in America is left to chance.

And it's this reign of mathematical necessity and this dynamism which frighten neighbors, enlightened by age, disillusioned by love, toughened by deceptions, a bit crippled by rheumatism. Where will these Americans stop, they wonder anxiously, while stirring the fire and pondering their horrible memories of war. They carefully observe America playing with the eagle's thunderbolts and juggling all those stars.

Faced with their colossus of an offspring, America's elders have succumbed to second childhood.

*

* *

"Give me your tired, your poor,
Your huddled masses yearning to breathe free,
The wretched refuse of your teeming shore,
Send these, the homeless, tempest-tossed, to me:
I lift my lamp beside the golden door."[32]

Wonder of wonders! America is inching along oh so slowly, slapped with taxes at every step, searching for a manageable system. The reforming spirit of Figaro emerges from his favorite haunt, slinks down the street and infiltrates many social welfare organizations in order that those consoling words of the statue will ring true for everyone.

"I lift my lamp beside the golden door." The Statue of Liberty on its island far from the Old World, close to the New World, becomes significant; it's a mistake to demean it as a mere tourist attraction. Even as a stiff statue, Liberty deserves respect, especially when she lights the

32. I have quoted the poem by Emma Lazarus.

way into the lair of gold, her light like the dawn of a new day full of hope for those who have come ashore in America with their bundles of dreams. She stretches to lift her lamp very, very high so that no person can be trampled, crushed, wasted in the America that Europe sees as a pedestal for man—Liberty lighting the entrance of a truly new world.

Sadly, America has not yet managed to lure Lady Liberty ashore; she has taken shelter on her island, as if to announce that she is still boycotting society, especially those who, protected by masks, can commit any crime by calling themselves a devil, a wizard, a master of the invisible empire. Is the American a coward, always requiring a mask to act, a hood to hang blacks, war paint to dump tea? If so, what is his true identity, the one finally allowing him to be labeled, definitively classified on a scale of values? In the present circumstances, even he could not articulate it. Politics demands that an aspiring candidate for mastery of the world not say exactly what he thinks. Effective as it is, this camouflage can't cloak the harsh light of reality, so the caretakers often have to use their sticks to prod their herd into the straight path. Numerous German Shepherds joyfully assist: do they not help lead the flock toward some roundtable or another?

The most blatant sign of the mingling of individuals and classes in America is the love affair between department store and pharmacy. To link firms and consumers, to make partnerships and place the miserable beside the happy is to link hearts and wipe out barriers. But what would become of the inhabitants of this nation if they awoke one fine morning to find the One Way had vanished, or that they had changed orientation or appearance? It would be the greatest catastrophe in the world, and the person who could accomplish this feat would have pulled off the most marvelous of coups. Imagine throwing a whole nation, even extraordinarily powerful and energetic America, off track by messing up the directions and colors indicated on the control panel—reversing the carousel! Who would not feel like a bewildered stranger in his own house, street, and town? Here is certainly the origin of resistance movements springing up around the world. Americans think of everything. To avert catastrophe and subvert resistance by making the world a witness, America nurtures the seat of the United Nations, whose influential and prestigious members all use the One Way. Since they would surely be quick to cry foul, no one will try to play this happy trick on New York for fear of having the whole world on their back.

To house the United Nations is to convene many disciples of the new great power, to observe them at leisure, to form their tastes and prime them for the task of comprehending all the nitty-gritty of the oiled mechanism which is American existence. This mecca of modern culture needs numerous pilgrims from every corner to be sent forth as enlightened believers.

Some travelers along this new road to Damascus prefer to remain doubting Thomases even in the face of the clearest evidence of America's super vitality, but just as the early skeptics changed into saints, so will his contemporary disciples. Under her huge eagle wings, America will henceforth welcome only saints and angels, singing her praises in chorus. The new Eden will boast its Saint Peters on which to build temples to the new white god, but the wrinkle is how to conciliate his demands with the precepts of the Bible, where America seeks daily sustenance. A machine will likely come to the rescue so that nothing embarrasses the United States of America. Although the master of iron and steel, she often lacks the cunning of the Old World, experienced in court intrigue. American citizens exhibit that candor permitted by the privilege of belonging to the richest country in a world, where wealth determines worth. No beggars, they can look others in the eye; even poor American citizens feel important.

The carousel of lights, storefront signs, road signs—all testify that Americans are deliberately opposed to moderation. Isn't it difficult to be moderate while measuring six meters with imperial feet? The American foot is a giant's foot. In this country of weaknesses, selfishness, and dreams, among so many unleashed desires, it was, of course, time for a new system of measurement. And since Americans have a different system, people treat them like alligators. Obviously influenced by the climate, everything here has developed toward excessively strange proportions: heads, eyes, teeth, legs. Piles of gold have become heaps; huts, skyscrapers trying to be new Jacob's ladders. Americans only recognize themselves as American by these particularly revered signs in order to better differentiate themselves from those they intend to seduce. Every American is a fisherman of hearts and souls.

To draw this colossus with feet of gold, star-spangled top hat, claws of a grandmother wolf, and a Mephistophelian beard is to equate him with the devil. But America has crossed this first threshold, has even gone beyond being the siren who sang to attract her victims, so she no longer hides her hand, certain of winning every point. She no longer seduces but orders—and everything works. A magic circle, where everything is moved by simple willpower. And the whole world is preparing to dance when the maestro gives the signal.

America plays animal tamer to the beasts of other nations.

Given the lucky stars America was born under, imagine what a beautiful destiny she could have had, what a sublime model she could have given the world! Remember Pierre Minuit,[33] who bought Manhattan? Well, America has missed the significance of his name: midnight; as usual, she can't transcend the superficial. No wonder America loves cement, scrap iron, and concrete, palpable material things like gold and the dollar, the unworthy masters of men and nations, hopelessly and desperately entangled, bunched up and clinging to each other to better withstand the inescapable pace. On her rocky shores, she builds modern temples to the aggressive yellow god. Midnight! The precise moment of the birth of day, the midnight of Renewal, of Renaissance, of victory over despair, brings only the same cries and horrors heard and felt simultaneously in old Europe. These same stresses people were trying to flee have here proliferated in an extraordinary way, like snails during the rainy season. Americans haven't been able to get rid of their European rags, clutching them at their breast like religious relics. Thus, the baffling, jarring, incongruous image as they attempt mergers between gold and Scripture, milk and tea, Coke and wine. These mixtures will free hands and cool heads to serve as peacemakers, because America seems suddenly to have realized that civilization is not the B 58, the blaring Chevrolet billboard on top of a building, or giant spotlights in front of theaters—overblown, pretentious, and tinselly imitations of old Europe. Only when Lady Liberty sets foot on the mainland will America really be America, home for the wretched, with room for all dreams, all melodies, all colors.

But who is to say that the Magus who feted Jesus with gold at Bethlehem was not really American!

*

*   *

It's a profound illusion to think that Americans hurry. From afar you might think so, but close up you see them walk calmly, all a product of highly developed limbs which give them an advantage over other competitors. They gallop. That verb might seem inappropriate as you

33. Peter Minuit acquired the island of Manhattan from the Algonquin Indians for sixty guilders and changed the name to New Amsterdam. He later became governor of Delaware.

enter one of many stores always swarming with customers and you hear only sounds of clogs, crumpled paper, and machines that collect, calculate, and return change—a full military operation, since trade has become another atrocious war waged against internal and external enemies, a never-ending war of hand-to-hand combat. No room here for the weak, idle person. No one comes to America to lounge about or to lick wounds, but to earn a living by the sweat of his brow or with the machines that have taken over for blacks. If anyone sits down, it's only to eat and drink, to refuel. And you had better be quick: behind you other consumers are waiting, trampling other pilgrims. Music plays everywhere as if to cover up the cries of those being crushed. America is a great country for music: record stores overlap perfume shops, perfume being as intoxicating as the soothing music for suppressing fatigue and promoting efficiency. A country furrowed by who knows what rains bares all the wounds Europe was trying to hide. A people in the process of overthrowing or recasting values to gain a new dimension. American music is open-air music, fit for the prairies where people holler and hail each other; noise to signal your presence, to build morale; noise for troops heading off to the front. You see, male and female singers howl and squeak during their repertoire, as if walking on rattlesnakes, urging everyone to quicken the pace since there's still a way to go in this lap of the race.

In America people also sing to lift spirits and, judging by the intensity of the sound, you have a vague idea of the enormous distances separating people and towns. The distance is so large that people rarely shake hands. Whether morning or evening, it's enough to say "hello!" for ships in the night passing and greeting each other! Eagles with huge wingspans refusing to shake hands for fear of losing a few feathers in the act. All this is enough to make us wonder whether traditional education is not in the process of delivering babes to voracious wolves; whether the world isn't a brothel for high-flying pimps—so much so that Americans with a refined sense of smell have already begun to be standoffish in their own country. You wonder whether the role of certain institutions isn't to create people thrilled with the idea of being forever sacrificed. Is Liberty in exile from America, deported to her island prison, surrounded by water? Not even Americans, who love to play cat and mouse with victims, would agree. These modern knights love money so much that it breaks their heart to give change. They entrust their machines with such draining tasks; thus they soothe their nerves, avoid dirty hands, and can look others in the eye. It's said that

Americans fix you with an astute grin but it's a silent interrogation asking: "Say, do you always return the correct change?" Thus Americans are so grateful to machines that they destroy homes in order to build multistory garages. It keeps the unemployed sleeping on the streets because rents are excessive. And some people dare wonder if machines will save or destroy America. A ridiculous question! The gods always save their creatures.

An American is very cordial when you climb over the wall of buildings into his heart! From the first day you meet, he always offers the opportunity to cross over by asking to be called by his first name, then giving his address and telephone number. And he will always hail you first: "Hello! Dominique!" and slap you amicably on the back. He's not being condescending because of a strong currency: the backslapping is a sincere, warm gut reaction. He will lead you to friends, who will lead you to acquaintances, who will lead you to their relatives; everyone will give friends' addresses. Parties will be given in your honor. America sizes you up on all its scales before catching you in its toils. Before pulverizing you in her powerful coils, like a boa, she runs her tongue over you several times to make it easier to swallow you. She puts you in a position of leaving her hell with some regret. Hello! You have only to fall into step to enter the One Way. Solitary people have no place in America, where you have to arrive heart and pores open. Relationships easily snowball as if Americans spent their time relying on each other and looking for each other in their many tunnels. Even so, in every shopping area there will be someone to relieve you of a few dollars so that you can have the appropriate relaxed look. Always maliciously mocking, he will watch you take out the dollar—at least here's one you won't be taking away he seems to be saying. America for the moment does not limit the amount of currency that can leave the country, armed as it is to wage war on every field in the world.

The dollar is exceptionally versatile, practically melting with sadistic joy in foreign hands. It's as slippery as the hordes of believers in the One Way. Not downplaying its demonic side, the dollar has as a sign an S slashed vertically by two lines, like a devil's horns. But you hardly notice the sign, the sound of the word itself is so alluring. To those who say "do-llar," it evokes a musical passkey which unlocks all hearts for America, as it charms, captivates, lulls consciences. If it is pronounced "doll-ar," it suggests the deceit and wiles of a coquette who deals in illusions. I discovered all the cute tricks of the national currency during my trip: it slipped away time and again for one tax after another. My hesitant, broken English hardly reassured it: national currencies do tend to be chauvinistic. This one demands a new red, white, and blue wardrobe Made in America for any travel abroad. It does not brook deceit, this proud and arrogant currency with its mustache and gorilla-like hairy chest—a purebred show-off. Without it, would there be any Empire State Building? Is it not the underground river quenching the thirst of all America? The dollar shouldn't rub shoulders with poor foreigners! Such a grande dame demands flowers, adulation, and obedience at the drop of a hat—demands I find monstrous. All set to believe that money was serving man in America, land of enlightenment in every domain, there was more telling evidence that man has become the servant of the dollar. America takes the wraps off everything old Europe means to conceal—yet another cause for misunderstanding.

Finally, let's not forget those people who pierce the S of the dollar with only one line: to them two lines seem to suggest crutches, obviously superfluous!

To understand America, you must grasp this symbolism of the dollar: its crutches help support the crushing weight of buildings, charities, fast-changing fads, powerful interest groups, and many satellites. Just as under the empire of Charles V, the sun never sets on the American empire!

America's governing principle that everybody and everything has a price is doubtless false: I tried to buy a heart in vain—even on sale. Can such hearts as I know back home be found here—ones that are calm, patient, maternal? Stuffed with sweets so that everything inside "burns up," American women resist you with an enigmatic smile which frightens even the boldest dollar. Could they be so enslaved by ancestral principles, old taboos restraining their hearts that they do not like to share a man's love? Such selfishness! The poor dears—if they had gone to school, they would know that the heart is naturally divided and you can put a lot of affection in its four sections. Muslims—very wise and pious people—fill the auricles and ventricles; they know a weighted organ works better. But Americans see things differently; they doubtless have a very weak heart and think they impress their wives by their height. Women laugh about this in that beautiful way only women have when they expose men's faults. Has a tall physique ever frightened a woman? Does she not have an atavistic fear of towering forests that simply burn, that spew out nothing but smoke and ash? Not good for the home fires! Women seem solitary; malicious men offer TV, but the women have grown tired of watching, so they've decided to work on their figures, which they guard jealously. Mothers of large families who live on the farms seem out of style, especially since men became navigators, travelers, discoverers. Modern young women, reared on cow's milk, look ahead boldly to the future. Aren't they a part of this America that's already writing off the "Harlem Globe Trotters" because they've discovered the secret of producing even taller men?

When married, they prefer to be in the driver's seat—a sign of freedom. There are numerous women on the highways who drive their husbands. If they happen to hit the curb, it's only in backing up; that's why men, who trust them, blindly abandon themselves into their hands—hands that can soothe the wounds they inflict. Besides, it's difficult for women not to rule over men's minds when they've placed under their care most of the disciplines taught at universities. When women drive, men close their eyes. Who knows why? On the other hand, a man has only to take the wheel for his spouse to worry: she constantly eyes the road and the driver as if to study his reflexes. Women know that a man at the wheel is a dreamer. Just let her son replace her spouse, and she recovers her calm, her color, smile, wit, and vitality; he is actually her blood, so she has confidence in him. So if you see an American woman sleeping in a car, it's because her son is at the wheel.

Do not be surprised by these contradictions; this is the country where most of your time is spent doing what's not to be done and only rarely what should be. What is done is calling a bakery Versailles, a restaurant the Elysée and spirits Bourbon—obviously because its power goes to the head so quickly—and building a "church" between two banks—that makes three temples—and many other things that are done but shouldn't have been.

Considering the plague afflicting everyone in the world, it's possible to assert that America, a blast furnace producing corn, apples, and capital, is only a vast shipyard for the new dynasties that are polishing up their weapons here. It's America's high tide, soon to reach its apogee. But what will it leave in its wake? Starfish, machines, and buildings, just as the "Portuguese" did when withdrawing from the shores of Africa and elsewhere; they left forts dedicated to all the saints of heaven. Such is life that all streams eventually return to their beds after having at the same time ravaged and fertilized the land. Although familiar to us, this traditional perspective on things seems to totally escape people here: when they observe the moon, they think only of its light—a very practical people, in this way, like their European ancestors.

But who in our contemporary world isn't like a European if only in his haste or his way of approaching daily problems or other people? Forcing us to realize to what extent people have stratified themselves in this era of commerce, America would like to have every heart won over by the Bible as well as technology. But she seems to remain too European at the core to make this last dream come true. Europe denies and rejects her; nevertheless, she can't say that Americans, except blacks and Redskins, didn't come from her bosom or leave her shores. After a long separation, who can always recognize a child who has grown up too fast? Europe can be excused and should be merciful to America, who still remembers and at every opportunity behaves like a good Western offspring—undoubtedly a little muddled from an excess of high spirits and never losing sight of her own interests. Would she be the new great world power if she had acted otherwise? What nation at its peak does not consider itself the brains and center of the world?

Prematurely gorged with gold, America is painfully stumbling along in search of the man she wanted to rehabilitate; but in what guise will the new man made in America appear?

*
* *

The airplane had to be invented to join such large spaces and allow Americans to save time, a carefully hoarded commodity of which any surplus will be canned for export to countries where this precious product does not yet have the clout it deserves. We're finally going to have time, to consume time. Surely that will help us escape all blind alleys and whiten us in the eyes of those powers that have a horror of a certain skin color! In eager anticipation of this happy event, clouds flock together sheepishly and are probably led toward some strange slaughterhouse or to some even stranger factory by people who want to lose nothing of their own free will.

The American no longer knows what to do to keep his lead since the country already produces bean poles. In these impeccably clean airplanes, he provides every passenger with paper bags, saying "For airsickness." Could American air be too strong for developing constitutions or for old organisms? These bags are made in Philadelphia: it took this wise, selfless, human city to think of those who do not yet understand the very expansive language of this country. And sugar, American sugar, has been so indoctrinated, so idolized and chauvinistic that it refuses to sweeten the bitterness of the coffee served to a foreigner. The authorities know it, but what can be done against stubbornness. The stewardesses know it, so they prefer to serve coffee without sugar, lest one of these devilish products cause diplomatic incidents. There are so many blacks traveling on American airlines! A true invasion. America seems to parade blacks through all her cities in order to get used to them. Some people will thus be able to realize that American blacks, products of the land, are not a strange phenomenon. Like all other citizens, they've been transplanted and, because of this, have a right to equal care and treatment. And so the astute stewardesses, to prove their magnanimity, serve you coffee with a very gracious smile, which makes you forget the sugar since it sweetens the beverage. As soon as they no longer have their feet on the ground they rediscover their feminine look and smile, even blushing a bit when you show them your teeth, I should say when your teeth show themselves in a smile corresponding to theirs. I'm bitterly aware that only a language separates me from these blonde creatures, no doubt chosen in a competition. They don't all catch this slight subtlety, but who can always claim to be aware of every nuance? Ah! if women wanted to listen to everything men say, guess everything they think, they would age prematurely. Fortunately, they lump them all together in the same basket and try never to anger them. And in order to have the courage to keep out of the way of those who make advances, they have secrets which they exchange, for example, changing sidewalks, neighborhoods, apartments. These unfortunates can neither give their hand to the first suitor nor go out with the last. Traditional religion and education are strict on this point. What is tragic is that one is always either the first or the last. In the long run that becomes annoying.

If Americans conquered the heavens and the earth, what would be left for others?

*

* *

What a compelling experience to be among people with whom there is no language in common! Each individual seems to be a smoothly glazed moving fortress. Individuals elbow and bump each other in an immense placer mine, some looking for gold in the earth's belly, in men's bellies, others looking for the same gold in the products of machines and the filth and blood of men. And all of that goes and comes, sings and dances, laughs and produces ingenious little runts who are completing the beautiful human cycle. Men have become like fallen gods who no longer even succeed in valuing or appreciating themselves. Cannibalistic gods! This is what I'm now experiencing among people who constantly have colds, whether it's hot or cold. They claim it's their way of talking.

I feel my way along, eyes wide open along the interminable corridors of "airports," going from "exit to exit." At every junction, I have to stop to see which exit's most crowded. Sometimes there are arrows, but they're American—what could be more silent! People at least make noise, and getting lost together with the natives shows the intelligence of a foreigner. God bless the man of genius who, for the protection of tourists without the language, thought to place all Americans in the One Way! That led me toward a taxi driver who ended up understanding that I wanted to go into the city. It wasn't enough to understand, so he had to embarrass me with "wheres and whats." A people of impoverished expression, who never seem to want to get out of the "wheres and whats"—the only words I understand in the mouths of men, women, and children.

*

* *

A surprising country, America, where no one talks about neighborhoods, color, barriers, lines, discrimination—but about compass points—notably East and West. The railroad had to come in order for parallel ideas to sprout in people's minds: this diabolical machine destroyed the concept of America. Yes—it's the railroad that divides Americans against their will. Aren't they all from one side of the track or the other? "The other side of the tracks"—it's a little like being at the right hand or left hand of God! White Americans insist on this subtle distinction because they too are from "the other side of the tracks." So, is there such a thing as barriers? Shame on the nation for assuming that men whose ancestors fought together for independence should be separated into white and black ghettoes, just as in the African territories. What it takes for black Americans to jump the "tracks" and be on the white side is a bank account, one fat enough to pay the extra rent required for access to the other shore—a toll. Nobody puts one over on the American ship of state! Radar in every corner spies on potential sneaks. Does America have a monopoly on this type of situation? Where else do blacks, like schools of fish moving upstream, displace other citizens in their march? Leaving behind Morningside Heights, they've reached Harlem, the Bronx, Brooklyn, New Jersey, Greenwich Village, and the waves are still growing: a terrific invasion! Having taken root in the New World, the real black peril condemns Americans to go around and around about the thorny issue of color. What if a man scorns your death threats and curses? Well, you can drive him crazy by wishing a black neighbor for him. Certain circles regard blacks as interlopers and bogeymen, very contagious through blood and mentality. That's why so many people walk around with a magnifying glass in their pockets, to look for the drop of black blood in someone who might have contracted it unknowingly. It's worse than the plague. As soon as a drop of this blood falls into a neighborhood, there's a rout. The black man per se isn't dangerous: you can approach him, touch him, talk to him, make him play and sing, even applaud him. You can observe him laugh out loud, sticking out his teeth to prove they're not sharp, but all the trouble you can get into with him comes from his drop of blood that distorts everything.

Certain travelers in a hurry to get back home maintain that the black question is purely economic. They've only seen restaurants, hotels, and airports, with their colonies of blacks. But elsewhere, in other areas of America, there are blacks who are very rich but who remain in their own neighborhoods. In their sumptuous houses, these blacks act as superior as whites on other continents, who swallow other whites along with a sprinkling of blacks. Who can claim that money doesn't give man an inflated opinion of his own worth? Here we can find a partial explanation of American racism: white becomes a superior color because it originates from the yellow of gold and the brilliance of steel. A very indistinct color, which doesn't always dare to assert itself but prefers to gravitate between the two poles: the somewhat milky white found in certain women and the white which, with time, is pigmented with black spots—the latter being the white which blacks have observed too closely and which keeps its traces of evil.

How can people who have the evil eye be loved? And these people have a capital, Harlem, a black town among white towns! Forty million evil eyes—enough to frighten those other angelic Americans! These blacks look sweet and hopeful but, all of a sudden, lash out like a stormy sky as if, suddenly, like water welling up, all the tragic past and present surfaces. Twenty million in less than a century! An evolution for some, a deluge for others. Such black endurance is alarming, considering the abysmal depths of their beginnings. Twenty million with no new arrivals! How many would there be if they had had the benefits of other immigrants? If they had lived in normal conditions? How many would there be tomorrow if their conditions in life were improved? This simple calculation terrifies American whites, black-vote seekers. How can anyone who thinks only of singing and dancing be a dyed-in-the-wool American? Blacks live an exciting life, do they not? Who could keep them in harness? The American straitjacket does not suit them, so as soon as they break out of U.S. grounds they can be themselves. For them it's an escape.

In factories, beside whites, they seem to be more relaxed, to have a prouder bearing. Are they not in the new cotton, tobacco, and sugar-cane fields? Being black in America becomes the label of a class, of those not able to be shown on television screens or in storefronts; their color would certainly scare customers away.

New Vulcan working with tons of incandescent steel at the ironworks, playing with sparks and flames which seem to obey him and bow to him, he produces the riches that allow others to dance the minuet, whereas he looks on from the street. Is the minuet one of his native dances? After having visited factories, it can be said that there are black sweat and white sighs on many American cars, and so the motor coughs like those who made it. Always at the peak of production, blacks should finally be able to get out of the guts of factories. His chains are no longer on his feet and hands but up higher, near his neck and head, and they no longer require more than a gesture, only one, ever so precise, ever so timed! Thus the problem of color in America comes down to the banal question of birthplace: one side or the other of that scourge of a railroad. And Americans are conscious of it, making a special effort to develop their air network in order to remove all the tracks separating neighborhoods and men. As a result of observing black clouds that send rain and studying the fertilizing properties of black earth, they've begun to wonder whether, when God judged that the time had come to populate the earth, the first man created might not have been black! That sometimes upsets these citizens—those very religious men who think that the order of creation was as follows: blacks, yellows, whites. God had reached the bottom of the earth, the limestone. How can that be reconciled with the story of Ham and Canaan about which Americans now seem divided? A notable evolution is taking place in them, making them much more open-minded—a fortunate sign for world stability and man's future fate. To elucidate this fact of ancient history, they undertake long trips to every country of the world. Could they be new explorers? After the Portuguese and English forts, the French barracks, and prisons of all nationalities, what does America have in store for Africa? Going everywhere in a whirlwind, these men have a morbid taste for the airplane. When the spirit of the machine enters its trancelike state in order to lift or lower the flying boat, he hates to smell the odor of tobacco. But since blacks spent their entire childhood and youth producing tobacco, they've retained its odor, some even its color. And so, for now, they're relegated to sweeping waiting rooms and carrying bags in hopes the spirit will get used to their smell. But these blacks, not understanding the spirit's prohibition, keep on smoking to scoff at their white brothers and to brave the wrath of the god of airplanes. All of these attitudes disconcert and disappoint well-intentioned white Americans, since the problem of containing the growing black tide has become almost impossible to solve. After the resounding failure of every scientific method, they had to turn to magic and sorcery, constituted of very powerful secret societies like the KKK. The leader took the terrible name of Grand Wizard, Emperor of the Invisible Empire. Unfortunately, there comes an age when you no longer believe in Santa Claus or an emperor. And so disdainful, derisive blacks now share a laugh about all the wizards and go ahead and smoke their cigarettes while waiting for a plane to bring its load of baggage to carry. And here the simplicity of the American soul bursts forth in all its splendor: keep the Bible at the bedside, miss no sermons, respect the Sabbath scrupulously, and accept being part of the phalanx of the Imperial Wizard! Americans aren't blacks, but there they are, also believing in the strange powers of a sorcerer. If a study on the sect of wizard-sorcerers had to be undertaken, it would have to begin in the United States of America, melting pot of beliefs and races.

*
* *

The long and interminable "airport" corridors lead me to a hundred-year-old university, where I meet one of the most famous Parisian writers. Will Paris never unload the heavy burden of leading peoples? Giving liberty was not enough, she had to control what was made of it. This Liberty, returning to France as stamps for collections, souvenir statuettes, or postcards, was a nightmare to her... was it possible to be so greedy! How could she make her loyal friend admit that, after all, Liberty is not to be sold like high octane gas or packaged like ordinary orange juice? Who could be sent on such a delicate mission? Who would be willing to clash head on with the powerful and touchy American dynasties, fix all the lights without being dazzled, hear the murmuring of banks and complete his task calmly while deliberately provoking fifty flashing stars? What new Goliath could grapple with the terrible American octopus with its iron, steel, concrete, and gold tentacles and gluttonous suckers? It was necessary to turn to someone dead. Ah! The living disappoint the dead, who seem to have taken away all the courage in the world. Obviously brave men have been dying for so long that we had to get to this point!... All the brave men who sleep in the shadow of a flag or a cross, all those countless lost men from slaughters coldly calculated to take a bridge or a hamlet, a hillside or a crossroad, all those heroes have, in fact, exhausted the supply of courage.

So, guess who I met here!

— Victor Hugo?
— No!
— Napoleon I.
— You haven't got it.
— Emile Zola?
— Yes, Emile Zola.

Emile Zola, here to study the new slaughterhouses, the new super "Au Bonheur des Dames."[34] He refused to rest, the poor titan, to sleep the sleep of the just. Because America is disconcerting, he insisted on rewriting another resounding indictment. There he is, walking, observing, studying the American phenomenon... To allay suspicion, to maintain the old alliance between the two powers, he has introduced himself here as having the features of a young African.[35] After such clear proof, how can it be said that Africans are wrong not to believe in nothingness?[36] This is surprising, upsetting all the scientific facts, all the European religious ideas. Go to the University of Ann Arbor in Michigan, near these interior lakes called the Great Lakes and you will be able to see Mr. Emile Zola, French writer born in 1840, died in 1902, revived in

34. The novel *Au Bonheur des dames* by Emile Zola is part of *Les Rougon-Macquart,* a series of realistic novels about nineteenth-century society. The theme of this novel is the battle between big business and small merchants.

35. Dadié is referring to a young student from Zaire whom he met while studying at the University of Michigan.

36. A reference to African fatalism.

1938. He is studying American humanities. How much hair will he still have in five years? The Americans, so precise in their judgments in similar cases, don't even know. Obviously how can they, frozen in their own values? In this venerable university, whose reputation had crossed seas and mountains, where I thought I would meet men filled with Holy Spirit, I've only found men speaking no other world language. For them, does the world begin and end at their borders? How do they conceive of other parts of the earth? So many points to clear up in a hurry! I asked for a glass of water without ice, and a man looked at me as if I had two heads. Americans can't understand how to serve water without ice. They smile, shaking their heads at such nonsense. I insisted:

— Yes sir, a glass of water without ice.
— What?
— What do you mean What?
— Who?
— A glass of water, but without ice.

Finally, the waiter caught on and with a broad smile leaned over the ice container to hand me—no! it was not for me but for the next customer. I had ceased to exist for him. I was a real pain, standing there like a lump, blocking the line. How could he serve me a glass of water without ice? My French ice had come out in English as glass? I fully understood his condescending smile. I wasn't a candidate for a degree from a university but from another place, a funny farm he certainly would mention (if he had not already) to all his friends who, after observing me in a queer way, left, nodding briefly. They had discovered a very interesting case to study: an African gone totally bananas. Their curiosity made the line longer.

Think how many wars men have doubtless unleashed for just such trifles! And so unrecognized heroes sleep: they who were going to fight for justice and the right to live, for the happiness of their brothers and then were crushed and sacrificed!

Fortunately, Americans don't espouse serious causes until after having understood them, that is, after having seriously weighed the pros and cons, they deem their future to be endangered. Preventive war to chase from their borders the flames that could burn their beautiful cities and blow up storage silos. This modern elephant goes out as a conqueror, sure of the legality of the war being championed. Angry at everyone who sides with the enemy, it's rare that a house remains or a country is not turned upside down in the face of a whirlwind, a tempest, a flood, another plague that disconcerts both men and the elements. Before Americans, buildings aren't burned, they're eradicated, demolished, just to avoid feeding their anger. This slows their advance, because finding nothing in front of them causes them to think. And for a conqueror, who knows how changeable the winds of fortune are, how capricious the fate of weapons, to reflect is to begin to realize that the same thing could happen to his own family.

The good American student didn't lose his temper over the ice and snow. American customs are beginning to soften and to differ from those we knew at Ndakarou[37] several years ago. Hallucinating soldiers saw fronts everywhere, at home, at parties, in the street: the street had become pampas and the citizens targets. They fired as if their country needed basins of blood to dye their stars that were too white. War was war, and it could and should be waged everywhere. The battlefield began from the moment of arrival. This image of the American with the smoking gun still remains in many memories, and it was often said of a boisterous child: "Oh, he's an American!" His excesses were tolerated out of respect for the great power of which he wanted to be a worthy citizen. He was getting in the habit of it, all the while chewing his gum.

*

* *

Welcome! declare doormats in front of doors and signs at the entrance of cities and towns. Nowhere do Americans teach you rules of politeness; they accept you as you are. America wants to be a haven for all. To come so far to visit, to face the anger of ocean winds, to run so many risks—all this certainly means that you didn't have enough consideration or an adequate hearing back home. She opens wide all her doors for you, certain she has the power to digest you one day. Of course no one likes New York, but everyone always comes back as if to attend an interesting boxing match: people roar and rustle, becoming actors in spite of themselves, caught up in the gigantic torrent of life, of movement sweeping everyone away—a collective hysteria, a voodoo dance. Maybe the African gods in exile are in collusion with Redskin gods to rule over American life.

37. Ndakarou is Dakar. After 1943, when Senegal rallied to the Allied cause in World War II, Americans helped build Yof airport.

*
* *

Every city should have its statue of Liberty since the love for Paris is undying. It's clear that Americans are willing to leave their isolation in defense of Paris. These men who should have had another name remember that they owe Paris their position as Americans. In fact, the name Amerigo Vespucci was given to their continent upon the advice, in 1507, of Martin Waldseemuller of St.-Dié. With no offense intended, it can thus be proposed that Americans are Italians overseas. If tomorrow Italy refuses to give Vespucci's name to this country there they'll be—awfully embarrassed at having to find another name after so distinguishing the first one given to them without any consultation whatsoever for the simple reason that they weren't yet a respectable power. Wisely, they still put feathers in their hats just like the Sioux, the Iroquois, and the Apaches, whose folk dances they carry off with astonishing brio; and just like them they eat corn, which seems to be one of their principal foods. In this way they want to get closer to the natives they've penned in, to study their customs and adopt them if need be. Customs in reserve.

But whether they're doing the corn dance, the hatchet dance, or any other dance, the Redskins consider the Americans' patriotic demonstrations only Vulture steps, which deeply offends these recently arrived Iroquois. Patiently they continue to eat corn to indicate clearly that they intend to evolve toward the primitive tendencies of the new continent in order to be its true children—a kind of renaissance that would link them more closely to the land and give them greater skill in scalping, for what they want is not so much to command the world but to be past masters in everything, to be the new leaders now needed by people. Such a role demands that they be in possession of all senses and faculties, and that is why an American will never say he is flabbergasted or that the cat has his tongue. He knows perfectly the story of the Parisians who, for millennia, have been throwing their tongue to every cat, who, with a wonderful logic, continue to mew the same incomprehensible dialect of Cat I. Cats haven't had the presence of mind to give numbers to their dynasty for the simple reason that men early on relegated them to the same position. And so none seems to want to emerge from the anonymous stream to become some torch whose name history would preserve. These devourers of Parisian tongues hardly appreciate torches—they don't like to be dazzled. This lack of logic on the part of the Parisian throws the American off—everything here, even the air, is conditioned! Would he remain silent for national interests or for other continents? Even more, who would plead his case eloquently if he made such an enormous mistake? Who would bestow any value on a speechless American? Can a people without a tongue be listened to? It's possible not to be Cartesian and know how to think... No, he will never fall in the trap of being silent. The question is debatable but how many would vote on it? For strategic purposes, statistics speak of one hundred and eighty-five million Americans. Official lie! First of all, what is an American and who can be American? These may be ludicrous, embarrassing, unanswerable questions left to individual wisdom, but they are questions nevertheless which must be answered to understand America and to judge her more seriously. Who in our time is not American? Who does not gravitate in the American orbit? Who does not catch himself daydreaming about the American dollar? Who wouldn't agree to go to Canossa,[38] to cry crocodile tears at the foot of Wall Street, tears which wouldn't fool those old crocodiles, the Americans, anyway. They've developed such a taste for goodies that every year specialists make them new teeth which they brush and scent every month. This gives them a most enticing breath. Others arrange their eyes and nails. These mild-mannered bosses take care of themselves in order to long remain impressive crocodiles. Along with sharks multiplying in every puddle and orangutans posted at every crossroad, they're a terrible plague for a country that can no longer produce small fry. Need I mention tigers, buffaloes, and lions that wipe out does and gazelles? the dangerous rattlesnakes you meet at every turn? A true fauna whose habits are worth studying in detail in order to know who can really be an American. Nevertheless, if it's agreed that everyone who obeys signals, who automatically stops or starts is American, it can be suggested that these are American: planes with one white star, missiles, war boats, radar allowing this country to read the clouds, TV, uniforms covering the warlike nudity of certain countries, all those America maintains to sing her praises—concubine states, boyfriend states, girlfriend nations, all draped in jewelry to attract all the other youth. All these are ready to back up America with all the tumultuous force of their voices; a decision coming from such a great

38. At Canossa, an Italian city, Pope Gregory VII forced Henry IV of Germany to humiliate himself to avoid excommunication in 1077. Therefore the expression *to go to Canossa* connotes surrender.

multitude of individuals could only be a monstrous decision, literally. It could be a family mistake, which everyone is obliged to defend, imposed as a temporary logic while awaiting the next "spare-part" decision. Might the American hurricane or the west wind blowing from Wall Street be trailing voices with a bad conscience? No one knows whether the national actors take pleasure in these tragicomic scenarios. Is it to encourage people to free themselves from their oath of bondage? To correct habits taken from here and there? Who can read an actor's mind, especially the American's turbulent thoughts? However, these actors have succeeded so well in their role that houses without records or books are rare. Music sustains conversation, fills in silences, and promotes reflection. A most surprising fact is the American affection for birds, a childlike love of caging these free beings and hearing them sing. Numerous stores have specialized departments for the sale of birds which, waiting to be taken away by some fine housewife or old bachelor, sing to encourage shoppers to part with their money. And what heart they put into it! Who doesn't put heart into serving the new world metropolis? How comforting it is to be the protégé of a great nation! Not only does she wipe your slate clean, she also encourages you in the worst follies, as if to give you a clear idea of the huge extent of her financial and political powers, and, it's rumored, with a generosity which ends up worrying even the greediest of her satellites. The milk America force feeds her friends is from Texas, and from Florida come inexhaustible supplies of riches. Florida and Texas seem to be the legs of the still shapeless monster which is the United States of America. Considered mature by some, America is still only struggling to establish her equilibrium in all domains. Even her greatest feats remain rough sketches, mock-ups. Since the results of mating with Indians and blacks has not been satisfactory, America looks to the purple man that Dallas laboratories will produce; newspaper headlines talk of nothing else. Wild crowds applaud the promising work of genetic scientists. Why agonize over these purple beings who might help solve the question of racism which has been entangling America for centuries? Why wonder when one James Watt, inspired experimenter, has done the thinking for several generations...

Watt? it's all clear. Everyone asks if you are a believer, if you think the experiment of the steam engine conclusive and complete; if the steam will go on to save the world or if the world will blow up like an ordinary boiling pot someone was having a good time messing around with. Watt? It's a buzzword.

You need enormous patience to study the American, a very complicated person, a person whom the telephone attracts and amuses. Everywhere signs announce: "It's smart to phone."

It's considered witty, intelligent, economical to phone. The telephone habit comes with mother's milk in a country where police sticks doubtless do not make it easy for truth to be told in gloomy basements of certain buildings. Probably America's sense of respect for the individual is too acute to succumb to the vile practices used in still-backward states of the world or in states which, just like children, hang on passionately to a past daily receding from their grasp. They need a reason for existence, proof of their strength, and these become the cries of children, tears of mothers, and groans of the elderly. They pound people as we pound rice in our villages, with a song on their lips. It's the ultimate sign of power. America, I've been assured, has managed to leapfrog this filthy pool in which sickly states flounder.

So if by chance you have to stand in line for a phone, be patient: look for a comfortable bed if you're behind a young man talking to his girlfriend. For him, nothing else in the world counts anymore. You could die of exposure at the door of the booth, and he would turn his back on you because "It's smart to phone." He'll stand there, glued to the receiver, munching "popcorn" to restore lost energy. The secret of American energy is in eating popped and salted corn, so well disguised that it could be taken to be bags of nuts.

Setting foot on this continent has the strangest effect: a man immediately feels made of entirely different stuff. He becomes a force, a torrent, a light, a general, a master-forge. To succeed in this gloomy forest, you've got to be well-armed to scare others off. And everyone knows it, elbowing in to upstage everyone else.

Who isn't a little bit American in this way?

Talk to an American about Paris, Stockholm, Vienna, or Peking, and he'll be embarrassed, because he won't know if you're speaking of his cities or others'. Murmur the name of Napoleon or Hannibal, and he'll listen carefully, because he also has a Napoleon, a Hannibal. This unfortunate confusion sours many relationships and creates painful misunderstandings. This allows people to say that America is committing suicide by claiming old ashes. Fortunately, men have been through enough so that they no longer fight over cold ashes, even famous ones. Therefore America can continue to keep her Napoleon and Hannibal without insulting the true heirs who bent under the weight of these giants. Didn't these phenomena protect people under their wings?

What other masters better than they could guide the steps of the young America on the path of glory?

What a great show to see Americans in the One Way of an elevator, the only place they look their best. Did they run the whole way there? Are they mute? What prayer are they silently muttering? Are they awake?—sleepwalking? Are they so calm and collected in that iron cage out of respect for machines? Who knows? Whom can they confide in some day? They arrive, press the button, and wait a few seconds; a click, then a gaping mouth opens, and they rush in. The mouth, now gorged, closes in on its prey, and there they are, off to a destiny chosen by pressing other buttons inside the elevator. Hands in their pockets, resigned, head down, they raise their eyes from time to time to read what floor the monster has reached. When the elevator stops, a bell rings, the mouth disgorges one or two still-silent victims, who scurry toward who knows what slaughterhouse. Willing sacrifices, all joyously accept immolation on the country's altar—beings forged by iron discipline to be winners. Even so it sometimes happens that they protest against machines, others, the boss—a silent, nonviolent protest. These are voiceless individuals. Protesters put slave collars on and parade in the streets, but hardly anyone pays attention as they come and go, stopping from time to time to obey that new army general, the traffic cop. Strutting with martial bearing, this man rules a kingdom of feet and wheels which obey his stick and, if he's prognathous, his chin. America's strength is to take man in the raw without claiming to correct him: people change themselves in America in order to conform. It's up to the individual to learn how to fit into a straitjacket in order to be among the elect, propped up not only by the richest bank in the world but also by the biggest fish market. Since those absent are always wrong, America insists on having a high profile, on occupying the best seats in any house. America's power and wealth constantly push her toward mountaintops—a nation suffering only the sweet vertigo of success. Her greatest feat is to have made you keep lifting your nose up toward the Empire State Building, Times Square, Rockefeller Center, and other dazzling edifices to keep you from "sticking" it into low-life sewers. The American beast lives in tiers, deliberately insulated by snobbism. At least American snobbism has different bases than the new snobbisms of new classes in new states.

You must from time to time venture into a "grocery store" to grasp how rich America is in all types of produce. How could you die of hunger in America? Hunger, no; indigestion, undoubtedly. Overwhelmed by the embarrassment of riches on the shelves, the consumer falls back on his hamburger. As for me, if I were a hamburger, I'd take a powder everytime I saw certain teeth approaching: better to be eaten without being terrified. Is it to dominate their hamburgers that Americans envelop them with their two hands? One more victim of the American appetite—so demanding and overbearing that most often people grab a bite at counters. One wonders why restaurants and drugstores don't close down.

Sunday is the Lord's Day, and money collected that day isn't placed with what is collected all week long: it's kept separate, to the left of the cash register, waiting for Monday to be blessed. Sunday collections in the various denominations worry Americans, who no longer know whether to give all or part of the Sunday take to God in order to render to Him what is His. Here we realize that all the shepherds responsible for churches and states work like blacks, allowing themselves scarcely any rest. They're always hard at it, up hill and down dale chasing wolves, and this chase sometimes prevents them from looking closely at their flock. They're pushing very hard against the boundaries of their pen. By erasing distances with their jet falcons, Americans unknowingly encroach on the territories of others, who treat her like an invader. After all, is she not the new guardian angel, armed with flaming sword on watch at the gates of Eden so that Adam and Eve never set foot there again? a new boss produced by the new world, a new open-minded role model? In this capacity, she dislikes having her feet on the ground, at ease only on the thirtieth or fortieth floor of her own mountain where she can converse with God. Every year she adds another floor to her Tower of Babel, wanting to be the first—noblesse oblige—to reach heaven and thank Christopher Columbus for the opportunity to fulfill herself and manage the world, which would die of old age without her. Faced with an information explosion, where does she gets the gray matter to churn it all out? You wonder, naively forgetting that Providence is an American city, that there are so many scientific advancements here that she can, from a distance, pick any brains she needs.

Trained to stick his head out of an elevator cage and to pronounce the magic words "up" "down" to put into motion a very secret mechanism in this new cave of Ali Baba, this man is the hottest rabbit in the world, considering that one hundred sixteen pilgrims landed in 1620, but after having digested the Redskins to avoid confusing figures, now, after three centuries, number one hundred and eighty-five million. That makes three hundred and seventy million arms, competitive links for American machines. And that's why they don't sleep: one hundred and eighty-five million hearts to cherish, flames to fan or to extinguish. Women appear so slender that it's a real miracle they've been able to survive such hellish exploitation. Crammed with milk and sweets, as white as they are, they truly don't seem to be worth two black women. American citizens refuse to admit these false equations of the Old World, and unwillingly they still maintain in music the relic of an age that didn't have the time to appreciate blacks. We can even wonder in what area white women are worth two blacks. Fortunately, men are reconsidering these inequalities, opening the doors of their heart to the full range of color, their mind enlightened, their senses strengthened to such a point that many of them, certainly out of charity, secretly practice the rotation of spouses. Knowing nothing of this, women do not cease praising the affection their husband gives them. Unfortunately, this system, flourishing openly where I live, hasn't become a part of the customs here, although the authorities, by taxing unmarried people, are engaging in a most praiseworthy effort. Used to all the hot temperatures, Americans laugh at the excessive zeal of the authorities: their resistance to "jumping" into marriage could come from the very selfish mentality of the women, who are more jealous than ours. Finally this delicate domestic problem that causes much spilt ink is submitted to the wisdom of a committee of experts whose conclusions everyone is anxiously awaiting. Nourished with the Holy Scriptures, the members of said committee will certainly remember that a very famous character from the Bible had two wives, like the African patriarchs. American women see the issue differently and consider a biblical age to be completely outmoded. History for them is a calendar and the facts pebbles that time washes along. No one really knows any longer how to take women, from which angle to approach them. You have to see them banging their fist on a table and crying: "Me. I want a man all to myself."

Cannibals and gluttons! Fearful by nature, men are rumored to look at women's teeth and belly before jumping into their arms. As for me, if I were American, I'd choose a woman with a very fat belly; that would give me several years' grace, a belly whose size I could oversee. Despite centuries of disastrous experiences, these citizens, who consider themselves very intelligent, continue to prefer flat stomachs. This has made all women hungry: they do nothing but watch their figure in order not to miss their "human dessert"—"A man for me alone!" You must admire the courage of an American husband who, while singing along, watches a boiling kettle. Don't you agree that he's on tenterhooks?

According to rumor, American women indulge in a true carnage of men, especially those gilded to the teeth. Great matches, beautiful prey, first-choice spouses. Men now have few gold teeth put in because they sense their species endangered. Truly I believed them of stronger stuff. To give in before a woman's threats and appetite tarnishes the glow of their crown a bit. Well, as for me, if I were American, I'd only have gold teeth: my words would carry more weight, all my lies and stupidities would be gilt stupidities and lies, and, therefore, valuable. People would weigh them with care, listen with delight, preserve them with piety, and follow them with enthusiasm. For I'd talk about gold for days on end; a new Chrystostom, I'd occupy all the major platforms of the world. Hanging on my words, fascinated by my teeth, no one would dare either doddle or doze with eyes open, even cough for fear of waking a neighbor who doubtless... Oh well, here's the formula: to make themselves loved, Americans should all have gold teeth. No more lips or cheeks for them; in exchange, they'd have the world's love, worth more than gold. Would they follow such wise advice if it came from one of their numerous oracles—the doctors? The importance of these leading lights in life, their influence on the conscience and mind is such that every American insists on becoming a doctor in something. Sometimes you develop a pale and wretched look, as you move about in the midst of all the white and black doctors who love to pontificate when they get the chance to explain their country. Just when you think they've finished talking after saying "O.K. Thank you," alas, they're only at the preliminaries: other people's time does not seem to count. You observe them consulting watches that never tell the same time as anyone else's. American watches are unusual; wearers never wonder how much time is left, but how much time they have to utilize and transform into action. Do they fancy themselves miniature factories? Only unbelievers and the naive demur: America takes too many liberties. Whose fault is all this? Where do the tyrants come from? Who produces them? What do you want her to do all by herself with that gigantic statue standing tall beside her buildings? Does she not, indeed, live in the majestic shadow of Liberty? Is she not the new capital of the world? And what metropolis ever did have any respect for the colonies?

Like latter-day Jesuses who want all the children and poor of the world to be allowed to come to them, Americans encourage me to learn their language, which I deliberately butcher to tease them. Philosophers, they first take a drink of milk to enlighten their mind and neutralize their mounting anger, then take me on again, calmly. A stubborn and discouraging patience. By reading the Bible, they know that God, after having created man, the modern monster, felt so exhausted, and was perhaps so disappointed, that He preferred to rest. He created nothing more. Well, he did create woman, but she wasn't anything new. Tired of protesting, they happened to become friends again with Rome; in this case, they preferred the leanings of a Saint Thomas, objective and unsentimental. But perched in the clouds of a fortieth story, Americans never lose touch with earthly realities: in fact, they hoist themselves to such a vertiginous height in order to better analyze them. Simon of Cyrene hasn't made any disciples on this continent either. Why help a god who wants to die by carrying his cross? For a god to die is hardly encouraging men to live, and it took this black Simon to understand that. What was he doing mixed up in this family quarrel? Whites were certainly crucifying a black who had become white to confuse everyone! If man were worth as much as gold or diamonds, why had God not hidden him deep in the earth? Who if not blacks had clear benefits from changing established values? Could such enormous and stupid contradictions come from the lucid minds of whites to whom earth offered real benefits? Abandon the earth for a problematic paradise? What white could be taken in by such a crude trick? Pontius Pilate washing his hands! Just another black believing he was cleverly extricating himself from the situation. Doesn't he tip the scales to one side by declaring himself "innocent of the blood of this just man?"

— Let his blood fall on us who want nothing of his paradise and let our paradise be Simon's hell.

And so that is why the second coming of the Son of God is delayed. What black will help carry the weight of the sins of the world? Who will play the strongman? Simon is especially criticized for having broken human solidarity, for having voted for Jesus at a time when all the votes went for Barabbas. He knew electoral habits thoroughly by dint of sweeping the polling booths! Let Jesus come back then! But Jesus will no longer return for the cross, and Simon still runs the risk of being exploited if he doesn't remain on alert. And after all, how could God send His only Son to kings who would legislate in His name, claiming to hold their powers by His grace? How could they be made to understand that all they had accomplished by proxy was null and void, indeed usurped? Kings hardly appreciate divine jokes which tend to bring them down to the level of ordinary men, their subjects. Jesus paid dearly for the courage of His father. Since then the world has been at peace: the example was salutary. No more god to come stir up trouble for men, to sow ideas that the earth can't yet handle. Distrustful, unwilling to lose on any scoreboard, Americans have chosen to transport Providence to their continent. What other paradise could be more marvelous than America with its chattering machines and its quiet women? Americans house God in America in order to watch over him: his ideas are subversive because they're unsuitable for the level of evolution of the human mind. And every morning they say secret prayers to Him...

"God, give me my job so that I can function like others, give me new feet so I can run around the world, give me courage to portray blacks on TV, and do not let women speak unless they're 'teaching.' "

I've very rarely heard the ingratitude of blacks discussed. Americans are perhaps unique among former slaveholders in tacitly admitting neglect: they know they owe blacks the greatest part of their fortune. These whites who do not seem to have helped Indians or blacks to develop could therefore leave the country with no regret. They realize this and therefore do everything possible in order finally to integrate blacks and Indians into the great family covered by the Stars 'n' Stripes.

America is finally waking up in order to give that initial emancipation act its full amplitude.

*

* *

American men mainly reproach God for having replenished His strength and recovered His bearings before creating woman and thus given her more resources than men, who were created after days of uninterrupted labor and they get revenge by making women work under inhuman conditions. Persuaded that it's for their health, their figure, women are beside themselves with joy, and men stationed in front of the elevator are responsible for caging them, for the "ups" and the "downs." Jailers, they stand guard in front of today's prisons and buildings. Women, brimming with eagerness, find men lazy as elevator control handlers: they relieve the men, one by one, thus releasing manpower for export—model workers for all the beehives of the world. In any case men hardly suspect the extent of the danger hovering over them. A disaster is threatening America: the second flood is coming—women. Will the new American Noah dare to take a woman on his ark; which would he take on board first—a television or a black? What role will the black play when he disembarks? So many questions come to mind when we look closely at the American way of life, when we analyze the help they can give to other nations. Are they alone in refusing to let states escape the darkness they're living in? Despite her fabulous riches, cacophony, and powerful vitality, America seems sad and only lives on the surface. And the most impressive fact is the silence of women in an office. It seems that men have removed their tongues to increase productivity.[39] It took the Americans to make such a breakthrough! So if America is growing at an astonishing rate and dazzling the world, it's because of the practice of tongue removal, a fine recipe for a polygamous culture. How could this citizen have come to such a practical, fruitful solution, having always been content with one wife? Now we understand why each woman wants a man for herself alone! She doesn't want to share her victim with others who might kill him too soon. To lull her victim to sleep, she likes to caress him on the cheek. She alone can be so bold with the American cheek, as wide as the world. And this immense and respectable cheek gets in the way so much that no one knows which one to offer in certain cases. American cheeks have become hypersensitive; the Cuban cheek covers decayed teeth, the Puerto-Rican, shrinking gums, the Formosan, teeth of undetermined length. Numerous trips throughout the world aim at finding spare cheeks. But America has so decayed mouths with goodies that everyone wonders which teeth might fall out under too sustained a caress. The feet of satellites seem full of corns, because each one on the tour takes precautions that astound the ballet master. Numerous are those that constantly observe the exit and approach it under any pretext. Fortunately, the boss is ever watchful, this man who, to respect the Holy Scriptures, will only go on a spree Saturday night, the Sabbath. Sunday he asks the Lord to give him enough strength to keep on going so that he'll be able to enjoy another binge next Saturday.

Here, then, is how this happy culture is evolving in its labyrinths of "One Ways," each illuminated by fifty stars whose excessive glare obstructs relations with other nations.

*

* *

The Roman Catholic Church, tolerated by Protestant charity, seems to be in a foreign country here. In addition, priests no longer have

39. A reference to the custom of the removal of the clitoris.

extravagant praise for American generosity. When a country has exhausted its supply of old billionaires looking for a young spouse, what's left to give to a world which has a material heart? America could now close up shop because she has no more hearts to offer, breasts to give pro deo. Knowing that, priests pass the collection plate twice. Americans have such respect for money that they've all become safes to be robbed. And so, by dint of hearing confessions, priests have ended up knowing the secrets of these walking safes. Their all-American technique is simple: require the faithful to act automatically. First test: onshore navigation. In the middle of the service, young men provided with plates circulate among the faithful for the collection of tithes. By the center aisle they return to the altar, from which they go out again for the big offshore haul, with long-armed baskets wherein people carelessly toss sealed envelopes and dollars. A joyous and holy rivalry takes place behind the priest. Understanding well that his Americans are sometimes very sensitive, this priest, in order not to influence any conscience or force anyone's hand, waits for the end of the collection to intone the Lord's Prayer, the Roman prayer, in which God is asked to give everyone his daily bread. Because of its community spirit, this prayer seems to be very popular with the faithful, who listen to it in deep meditation. Indeed, America is striving toward just such a conception of human relations. Quench all thirsts, assuage all hungers! What she will not tolerate is that others allow themselves to outdistance her on this path she's following oh so slowly in order not to frighten anyone away. In certain areas, Americans don't tolerate a disturbance, especially if the national interest is at stake. Newspaper vendors are waiting at the door to sell their news, to allow it to mingle with the priest's advice. What a huge experimental ground the American mind is; fortunately, almost everyone in this country is Protestant, for if they were Catholic, they'd end up having the Bible say that God first created breasts in women, then bottoms, and between the two, for balance, a body. Weaned too soon, perhaps not breastfed but nursed with cow's milk, Americans have maintained a morbid love of breasts. How can you avoid dreaming of breasts and bottoms when there are so many splendid ones in this country? And specialized magazines sold in kiosks take on the mission of exposing, exhibiting, and popularizing this other aspect of America.

Here another paradox becomes clearer. Americans set up quarantine lines around white women, whose nudity they peddle, to show blacks, if they doubted it, that all human constitutions are the same. Therefore, they prove that the rapes sanctioned by the Grand Wizard and his bloodthirsty clique sometimes cover up shameful motives and issue from an atavistic chase after one color. Isn't a person who can't manage to blush, even after centuries here, a monster? Don't blacks now understand why they frighten whites? But they're stubbornly attached to their color as if to a life jacket. And this despite so many choices offered them by the great democratic power, including what soap to use to whiten their body and face. America can't make heads or tails of the situation and would've thrown in her hand if that were the American way. What disconcerting beings, these blacks populating the continent!

*

* *

The peoples of color are unquestionably not black, yellow, red, but certainly white. And they're only white because there's no mark yet that indicates their quality.[40] Open your eyes and look! Look closely, observe ten white faces—that's at least ten different colors. But for whites these aren't true colors because they're artificial. Blacks, who confront whites and dispute their right to existence, know better. After all, didn't they arrive in the land of the Redskins before the Statue of Liberty and the other pilgrims? Haven't they worked this land with their hands, flooded it with sweat, populated it with dreams, and charmed it with songs? The color white is too fresh; it hasn't had enough time to stick to the skin! Whites suffer knowing this. The child's grown up and is no longer afraid of either the ogre or the Grand Wizard with his colored face. Now when the Ku Klux Klan makes its nightly rounds, American black kids clap their hands to make the Grand Wizard dance. They, too, have turned a page in their history.

*

* *

Don't be surprised if American women don't always smile, if they appear tired, overwhelmed, distant, brusque, nervous; theirs is a tragic

40. Dadié is referring to the comprehensive appellation contrôlée system, which is very important in maintaining the quality and marketability of French wines. He uses the French term *appellation non encore contrôlée,* in contrast to the *appellation d'origine contrôlée,* guaranteeing that a wine has been produced in a stated location and conforms to the rigid laws controlling production.

destiny, a family secret no one discusses for fear of losing respect. Candies, ice cream, milk, and buttered bread have made them so soft that men consume them in appalling quantities. Tenderhearted souls who love flowers so much that they put them in their hair to attract the males buzzing around, American women bear their fates silently. Who'd listen to their complaints? They have recourse to this strategy only when their rosy cheeks begin to fade. As for their hair, some women wisely take the precaution of tinting it white, thus rushing through the years without stopping, getting a jump on time, but flowers and white hair only make men more aggressive. Total silence and a most gloomy conspiracy surround this great slaughter of women, this certain destruction of a species. American lecturers, diplomats, and canvassers always speak of their good intentions, their understanding of problems, their objectivity, but never of what they do to women or how they "consume" them. Here, there, and everywhere—dreadful carnage. Women—mute, defenseless beings delivered to ogres! Look at all Bluebeard's boutiques selling women's heads, authentic heads wearing hats they wore before being cut off! These heads are bait. Crowds of women flock daily into these stores to beautify themselves while waiting their turn to have their head exposed in a well-lighted showcase. They say it's a great honor for a woman to have her head exposed there. Men have succeeded in killing all the glow in American women, who, of their own free will, proffer their necks to cries of joy and applause. Strange customs only Protestants can allow; if they protested, they'd become Roman Catholics. The logic of the situation chastens you, given the silence of Catholics who are afraid to protest for fear of being Protestants—a vicious One Way circle. For now, American women bear the burden of this new religious war. To escape their enemies, some—neck extended, chin out—walk so fast they scarcely leave any trace. Hunters by nature, men follow them, not by tracks but by scent. And women can't escape because these same male vampires make their perfumes. Their Machiavellianism is so strong that every year they launch a new brand of perfume for their victims to pounce on. The more women believe they're escaping, the more they give themselves away. To throw women off the scent, men pretend the exposed heads are wooden or wicker. Still they denigrate women. How can you say that American women have wooden or wicker noggins? America is not a very gallant nation— and that considerably tarnishes her reputation among other peoples.

Women know all this. As soon as they reach maturity, they find a true panther, leopard, or tiger skin and don it as a coat or hat. Terrified, men arm themselves and give kids revolvers as first toys. And despite all future protests from the civilized world, the future will still find women's heads in every shop window because America has acquired a taste for violence. After gold, machines, and grandeur, the One Way and the South, this infernal situation is America's sixth bleeding wound.

*
*　*

Conscious of their worth and their rights, American women prepare their revenge by playing an apparently innocent game: bowling. This game consists of knocking over pins with a ball thrown as hard as possible. Players shake hands, laughing. What a great pleasure it is to see them playing so joyfully, hammering the pins as if hammering the skull of someone who broke a promise, scattering them as they would a battalion of men. I ask you what individual would feel courageous hearing women yell: "I want a man all to myself." If I were an American Bluebeard, I'd already have kept my distance. But American males don't suspect a thing. They're too busy thinking of their bank account and their comfort. To save their necks, the most perceptive join the army and go abroad, where they continue to serve their country by producing little Americans. Very reserved at home, once out of his mold, they literally bubble. An American aboard—that makes fifty individuals, fifty stars that must be accepted and loved. Love conquers continents and barricades. American cuckoos lay eggs in every meeting-nest—bridgeheads for a peaceful conquest. Brought to such a difficult battlefield as that of a bed, war has lost the opponent. Only the marriage of stars remains for the pacification of peoples. The red male frightens all the white virgins, who dare not cross the threshold of the new ogre. What dowry could they bring? An economy based on high octane gas, waterfalls, freighters, supermarkets, superfortresses—a solid economy, enmeshed in mountains of gold and in offices controlled by overworked women who end up going crazy.

*
*　*

An American will keep on looking for years for a marriage partner since he's looking for a mother, not a mother-in-law, in a woman. The insensitive and vulgar will mention divorce. After running around all day, living with the noise of machines, he expects to be cradled, cuddled, to feel like more than a robot. And if a woman wants him to continue to play the same role as at the factory or office, divorce seems the only act of revolt and self-affirmation. America is the country where you can pursue a heart, literally, into court. Women know the insecurity of the man whose eye they've caught at a street corner or at a reception. They'd very much like to keep him, but what can they do? They're also American and, as such, give up no rights to anyone. People haven't yet understood that marriage is a bonding of two wills, the fusion of two individuals, which implies preliminary compromises. Far from being the cross some imagine, marriage only requires care. To care is to always put yourself in your companion's shoes in the least important actions and words. Will the preeminence granted women allow for concessions? Where will this notion of absolute equality end? Will men soon be consulting midwives? Riding a hobbyhorse of absolute equality, women would have you think so. Fortunately, many have understood their role and try to provide happiness for their children and spouses. In order to fully espouse men's ideas, women have also put feathers in their hat. There's no longer any doubt of kinship with the Redskins; women, the last holdout, have given in. Can we speak of reservations when everyone in this America seems penned in, limited, restricted? Redskins have other things to worry about than to go and reclaim remnants of feathers to be put in their hair. Americans are thus becoming Redskins. Many people claim that ceremony and style shouldn't be used as an absolute criterion of civilization. The same could be said of the American abuse of machines and their profit motive, which results in the construction of purely functional things. But America must produce money, not dreams. Dreaming is neither functional nor American. But is it only Americans who deny men their dreams? This universal lack of dreaming, even of sleep, makes certain people so tense and tired that they unwittingly tread on their neighbor. Totally mechanized in order to liberate man from all burdens, America is searching for a heart and soul, a truly human foundation: only then can the Clarks and Laurences, who drive the same make of car, be considered in the same boat. But for now, when David, back from the South, starts talking about his skirmishes with Goliath, who's enclosed in his white tower, everyone listens closely, scandalized. Despite all the laws, the South, for centuries mobilized for the war of colors, for this eternal checkers match where the black pieces always remain prisoners—the South, in fact, constitutes a disgrace for the whole nation. Pretending to be a grand wizard comes from the most juvenile of mentalities. The clearest sign of death is the absence of laughter. The person who doesn't laugh is dead, and America, through her numerous miracle workers, allows us to live. She deserves our gratitude because she exposes in broad daylight the defects of a civilization others insisted on covering up.

Has anyone ever claimed that America is populated by saints? A profusion of beliefs could only have led to the worship of infernal gods, who, from the bowels of the earth, watch over gold, diamonds, and other so-called precious stones—so precious that God made them before man and locked them up in earth's deep safe. Not being the first issue from the creator's hands, man is devalued: he remains the clay that all the world's master potters insist on modeling. Man—the toy young kids dismantle so they can see what's inside, the plant evil gardeners would like to see grow in a hothouse of squalid poverty, the only plot where money can strut its true stuff. Man—a marvelous invention, a passkey welcomed in factories, on war fronts, in sewers, throughout the cosmos! He knows that someday he will be asked to line up in a parade, to hear the acclaim of an enthusiastic crowd transform him into a hero. This will make him forget all his troubles. But it's a dismal scene—even for whites![41]

Lost in circuses and arenas, women are patiently looking for a companion with a heart. At the wheel of her car, she bears down on people crossing the street just to test their courage. The one chosen is the one who foolishly courts eventual death, who throws himself at her feet, because he's already accepted subjugation. Men, who never count themselves out in this duel, have turned for vengeance to haberdashers, who have good reason to have it in for women. Don't be surprised to see those silly, shapeless cloches on charming American heads, those concoctions of parrot feathers inherited from the Redskins, of guinea feathers, duck feathers, and chicken feathers—those divers' helmets designed for protection against filthy street water, those half veils Muslims like to put on their women to limit their intelligence and contain their passionate glances. Another male ruse that American women haven't understood. But never say American women aren't smart. There are doctors among them, doctors who act dumb on the subject of hairstyles. The American male is a dangerous magician.

41. The translation of the word *noir* in *un tableau noir* as dismal conveys the idea of darkness.

Despite massacres and humiliations, women continue to look for their hearts' delight. For many men, love is like those gas stations where you pull in, stop, telephone—the dish is served in ten minutes—you eat, pay, and pull out without ever leaving your car. Women want men to get out of their car, their shell, their American colors, to be open (the heart agrees), and whisper something storybook sweet. Dogged by all the cares that corner them in America, caught in the gears of American life, men don't have time. Women want a companion to love them, to embrace them; they want someone to whisper "I love you," but time is so precious that a date becomes an appointment. America is a country of large fortunes but not yet of great loves: the stuff of epics, not romance. Here you amass fortunes, which demand strength and wiles—but never love, which needs patience and wisdom. So a woman bridles her heart with a tourniquet limiting the scope of her exploits and style: men call her "miss," a contender who sharpens her weapons while demanding from them a long probation period at the foot of her heart. Since marriage is a long march, she looks for a good pair of boots: you never know where a chance leap can land you.[42]

*

*   *

— I'm very busy!

If women in other countries ever say they're busy, ask them to come here to see their sisters who live in the shadow of the august Empire State Building! They're dying from work; they're exhausted. They're on call night and day so men can have time with the children.

— I'm very busy!

In such a mechanized country, one wonders why women aren't finally free of chains. Living like common mortals would not be American, not for people whose baby teeth are still intact, who're ignorant of how to use excess energy. An iron constitution conditions and favors action: Americans welcome sweat as proof that everything inside is working. But who knows if machines are tired or not since they don't sweat. Those wise bosses have taken the precaution of placing clocks everywhere, of seeing to it that they ring loud enough to get through to the deaf. For this reason we still find Americans in America; otherwise,

42. Dadié plays on the word *bond,* as both marriage and leap.

they'd all be dead of exhaustion. Already their heart can no longer keep up with the heartbeat of machines. That's why a woman in this America of happy galley-slaves always has the look of someone marking time. Doesn't she intend to participate in her people's struggle? to enjoy its success? to get out from under the oppressive tutelage of men who've dominated her for so long? She'll be a citadel he must take by force. Prepared on all sides, she has an agenda:

Monday: work + appointments + invitation;
Tuesday: work + dentist + if + visits;
Wednesday: work + laundry + movie;
Thursday: work + studies + shopping;
Friday: work + perhaps + surprise party;
Saturday: work + I don't know + trip;
Sunday: church + maybe + but + relaxation.

A marvelously structured schedule she uses to test male skills, patience, and courage. On such a battlefield, the lovers' joust begins with what is called "dating," of capital importance in a country of such great loneliness that even television has no effect.

Dating gives a woman the opportunity to play with the heart and head of a man, to make him pay for all those heads displayed in shop windows. She drags him from gully to gully, level to level, lock to lock, falls to falls, roller to roller, through a long calvary that will forever remove any desire to have a woman on his hands. She keeps him in suspense, making him hope every day for an imminent surrender. As a matter of fact, it's the unsuspecting man who's under siege, ogled, sized up, and forced to confront himself—the woman always having the power to make him believe the moon is made of blue cheese and the ability to carefully lead him by a long leash while giving him the illusion of freedom.

Dating begins with the early boyfriend era—at the age when the glazed, hesitant smile fleetingly casts a glow on an indecisive feminine face and timid fingers, just as the first rays of a star illumine a formless void. At this stage in the relationship, securely ensconced as she is in the corner of a couch or crouched near the fire, don't bring her your mother's picture; she'll scarcely notice it, intent rather on sizing up your sacrifice, the immensity and intensity of your love, the length of your madness, the weight of your confidence. Her demeanor cooled, her mind confused, and her heart troubled, she'll keep tugging at her fashionably short and disobedient skirt, trying to cover her chilly ankles (the mirror of the soul). The moon could be at her feet and she'd scarcely see it: your feelings don't seem very orthodox to her. To improve your manners, overcome your devilish instincts, and charm you, she'll play several records, then yawn to end the meeting. She won't extend her hand; that's just not done and, moreover, since you're certainly the devil incarnate, the extended hand would seem like a pole. Finally she'll examine herself to see if you've forced anything on her, if all the barricades are secure, if the machicolation is in working order. Bye!

Following this heroic era of contact is the more defined "casual" era where you defrost a bit, thaw out. A feminine venetian blind slowly rises: the Amazon face softens, and flashes of a blushing smile persist in the corners of her lips and the wings of her nostrils. She observes and studies you from the corner of her eye. Who knows who's being chased? Her gestures become more rapid to chase away invaders. Lowering some drawbridge, she can now politely ask you to strike camp and raise the siege so that she has time to count her dead, regroup, and get her bearings.

Then comes the third stage: the friendly era—time to make time. She agrees to ask you questions.

— Do you like the United States of America?
— No.
— Why?
— It's too big.
— But wonderful.
— A very embarrassing and baffling country...
— Are you married?
— No.
— Why not?
— I'm waiting.
— You don't like women? Are you afraid of them? Who're you waiting for?
— You...
— Liar! What if you hadn't met me?
— I would have waited.
— How long?
— Until I met you!
— Where did you go to school? Con U?
— A man never lies...
— My God! Do you like to dance?
— Yes!

— What dances? The twist?
— Yes.
— Wonderful.

The twist symbolizes the rage for life sweeping across America today: a dance of the feet, hips, hands, neck, head—of hysterical contortions, lunges, and retreats. It loosens old instincts that were asleep, linking dancers to the soil where they seem to want to sink, a whole people held in its sway, struggling to cast off nets woven around them. Fortunately, it will last about as long as a new car, that is until a new craze pops up from the assembly lines producing soup, records, and new steps.

— Do you like football... the game?
— Yes.
— I like too... Wonderful!

Yes indeed, what devilish enthusiasm is displayed during a football game! Spectators yell, clap their hands, stomp their feet, scream, whistle, stand up, sit down, yell to each other, and throw their hats in the air. Everything in them is awake, alive, and moving. Americans want to have leisure time in order to make life a permanent holiday: here they create a new life-style, one that machines don't yet allow them to display. Their football, played with hands, is different from other nations', a kind of guerrilla war consisting of occupying the field inch by inch, foot by foot. The rule is to run with the ball and fall as far as possible with it to indicate the gain, the territory won from the enemy. Thus we see players rolling around on the grass with deep childlike joy, throwing themselves on each other, forming a moving pile of feet and heads that would stay there if the umpire didn't whistle. An untended goal. A line and a red flag indicate it. So now we understand the meaning of a quarrel. By sporting a red flag, which, in international law means "danger," Russia stands out to all firemen as the center of the fire, a volcano which must be watched. Being past master in the art of firefighting, the U.S.A. stands guard around a glowing red center.

Old Glory floating serenely above the excited crowd is reassured by the noise that America is still vital, spirited, patriotic, and pugnacious. From time to time, a Jolly Roger waved by a boy surges from the swell of heads, a sign of a fan's enthusiasm. A naive traveler, dazzled and duped by the gaudy signs and by the dizzying height of the buildings, might extol the astonishing American progress. Well, beware—America, home of bluestockings paranoid about world opinion and of country folks who have citified houses, unfortunately has not fully evolved. She is stuck on a plateau, behaving like Napoleon's Old Guard or the Imperial Guard during the Directory. She regresses insistently to past centuries as if afraid to face the present threat of being mauled, crushed, then annihilated by her own machines. Re-creating step by step French history, she wants to burn Moscow and suffocate England if a new tea war were to break out, rebuild the empire, and create the American dynasty. In the carousel of colors, Spain is the victor.

In her short existence, America has burned out. The child prodigy eager to play Hercules is now a new Atlas exhausted by the complex world of dilemmas other nations have placed on her shoulders. To play the role with dignity, she dresses her soldiers sumptuously. By this device she gives them a taste for life, that is, the understanding that they must always win.

These people, who wait for their "Romeo and Juliet" and their "Heloise and Abelard," carry a painful memory, the only one undermining national honor. What got into Frances Slocum?[43] What trail did she want to blaze for American women? How naive to think she could open a new path in a continent already crisscrossed with trails? In short, she was captured by the Redskins and she preferred their company to that of her brothers of color. Back then there were no psychiatrists, and no specialist since has studied this strange case. Just like Silver Dollar Tabor, she had no disciples because communities could not get involved without much too much risk.

If America lacks a Romeo and Juliet, a Heloise and Abelard, embroidery, laces, and the fine art of fan waving—even roses—it's because this country prefers to produce mastodons. Doubtless one day across the smoke of factories and the portholes of buildings, she'll see that multitudes of men are toiling painfully so that the national Star might shine more brightly...

Isn't American football truly amazing? Isn't it marvelous how they maintain the fighting, competitive spirit, which makes head, hands, and feet think?

43. Frances Slocum (1773–1847) was captured by the Delaware Indians at the age of five and lived among the Indians all her life. Her second husband was a Miami chief, and she was living in Indiana at the age of sixty-four when her relatives visited and she refused to leave the community. The mother of two daughters, she was known as the "White Rose of the Miamis."

Like a distant flash of lightning, a quick smile lights up the face of your conversation partner who's feeling you out with a malicious pleasure.

— Can you drive?
— Very well.
— Oh, that's marvelous! What car do you like to drive? Do you prefer American models! Why?

The last friendly test leads to that dangerous crossroad of "like and love": the first leads to a dead end and the second straight to the heart. You have to maneuver with exceptional skill between the gorges and reefs of the American heart; you have to play the game with such enthusiasm that the woman won't look at you and say "I like you but I don't love you." Those are the two brands of affection produced by the "cardiac" factory. The man who stumbles on "love" takes an easy tumble into affectionate arms. "Like" will stay in the waiting room, where it will be kept at arm's length and condemned to talk about the weather. He will waste away at this stage in the sentimental journey if he doesn't withdraw very soon. No one will ever say to him: "I'm tired, but for you..." Only tolerated, "like" will bear a crushing weight he'll be doomed to endure, and she'll only have to appear for the sun to shine, even in the worst of seasons. At this last stage, the heart of the American woman, like a balancing pole between "like" and "love," can get dizzy and go crazy.

What car do you drive? A seriously ambiguous and embarrassing question. What car can you drive when you're in America? The question was only a booby trap. Your silence saves you and advances you one level into her heart. You come off as a very intelligent man she can associate with. There are silences in love, smiles which reduce pockets of resistance and raise the drawbridges. When she's friendly, a woman consents to give you the tip of her fingers: the whole hand remains to be conquered. She can now accept an invitation but at the last minute will have a toothache or headache. She'll continue to pay some attention to you, notice the color of your tie and the sound of your voice. Slowly but surely, she forms your character and tempers it like American steel.

There you are, ready for the rank of "steady," that point when she gives you her whole hand, but her eyes will focus on the ceiling or the

TV. She's ready to be won over "and so forth."[44] America has fifty stars of different temperament, all found in women. As the highest honor, when the television is on, she'll put her finger on your mouth: silence, the new god speaks. Finally, you can call her; she will grant you a few minutes snatched here and there. You linger in her thoughts: now you are the "lover." You can eat corn on the cob together; eyes light up to sustain the conversation, illuminate it, guide it. Even the silence is eloquent and the room intensely heated. At this high point in the relationship, the woman can get up without excusing herself. Now, after such effort, after an assiduous campaign, you're part of the place, a household fixture she can sit on with the most agreeable of smiles, to avenge all those decapitations in store windows. The "lover" era naturally leads to an "engagement," a critical period in this seesaw. You can see her "anywhere and anytime." At this dangerous juncture, be careful that hand-to-hand combat doesn't lead to a Sedan or a Waterloo. You're in the stronghold and in charge. The woman becomes a "protected lady,"[45] hidden, veiled, insidious. You can go out together and remain alone, very alone, no matter where you are. All those couples seen walking together, avoiding pools of light, stopping from time to time to kiss, nuzzle, and nibble ears, are in the beautiful dreamlike period. They're fighters feeling each other out, looking for chinks in the armor.

Then one morning, impelled by who knows what devil, they take the "leap" into "marriage" with two "r's," an association but not a merger. The man fully earns the coveted, sought-after title "my dear," precious, pretty, nice, charming—the equivalents of my cabbage, my little rabbit[46] —all the names the heart ostentatiously attributes to the one who, tomorrow, will make it suffer.

"To make a good match!" To make a good marriage! To reach a goal. You've won the competition; you're a hero. But "dear" is not very far from "deal"—business, the market—or from "death"—the same word family. And since no one comes to America to die or give up rights, a man easily picks up the pieces of his character lost along the long journey toward the heart of his fiancée. The woman no longer recognizes him, so... No, in America you don't divorce, you separate. Mar-

44. A typographical error in the original text or a mistake in English renders the original *and so one,* translated as *and so forth.*

45. Dadié uses the term "feme covert" for a woman under cover or protection of her husband, an engaged or married woman.

46. French terms of endearment.

riage with an extra "r" contains the "R" of rupture. Couples split up and look for another port, another buoy to anchor their heart; you're in America, you can leave each other without divorce and you can divorce without leaving each other.

In a state excessively rich in subject matter, how can I describe women—these men germinated last in the mind of the creator and who are in the process of developing? They like you to approach the reef where they live; they like you to define the enigma they would like to be: it tickles them, makes them smile, and allows them to disguise their game even more. They constantly study the tricks of their assailant. You must acknowledge that they're sometimes very "wonderful" and that such a long siege becomes a joyous game of checkers for the man. That doesn't prevent him, however—when the game is too close—from asking himself the same question vexed lovers the world over ask: "What the deuce am I doing here?"[47]

Do American fathers, like African ones, advise their children to beware of alcohol and women? of all intoxicants? It seems their words fall on deaf ears.

For the big "leap," the woman dresses in white, the man in black. Already the difference in their tastes is beginning, only to be accentuated by time and differences in personality. When getting married, the man mourns his lost rights, whereas the woman feels sacrificed, delivered—white, naked, defenseless—into the hands of a person who's constantly hidden his game like a good dictator. While window "shopping," she can see into what depths she has sunk: all those heads and feet exposed, those fingers holding stockings fresh from the factory! A flash strikes her; a glimmer of indignation runs through her. She must let the world know the conditions American women live in. To do so, she'll carry out an extensive correspondence, but the stamps on each letter will belie what she says.

How could such horrors be committed in the shadow of the Statue of Liberty? "Of the people, by the people, for the people," a stratified trilogy reduced to a banal postage inscription destined for overseas. Would the happiness of the American people authorize such violence?

47. Dadié quotes the famous words by Geronte in Molière's *Les Fourberies de Scapin,* "Qu'allez-vous faire dans cette galère?" and then translates them as "what business had you there?" I eliminated Dadié's translation in quotes and rendered Molière as "What the deuce am I doing here?" to best fit the context. His translation: "what business had you there?"

Is this just a simple slogan like so many seen at political meetings? Even if it were true, if every American had taken a fancy to women's tender flesh, who'd be willing to cast a slur on the honor of such a powerful and generous state? Anyway aren't women made to be swallowed up by men? If the citizens on this side of the ocean allow bones to lie around, it's perhaps because women's are so hard that they haven't been able to munch them like so many others in the world. In a country where everything must serve a purpose and make a profit, they've made them into props for hats and gloves. Always up to date on new American trends, aren't other nations soon going to follow her lead and make bones profitable? just as they've enthusiastically adopted the rubber police billy club? America likes to do things correctly. The rubber billy club dents the head without making it burst, and it never wears out! It puffs up the skin without ever drawing blood. Clean hands always! And to prove it, letters stamped domestically spread the image of the White House and the portrait of national heroes so people will know and appreciate that they're a people of heroes, supermen—consumers of the Bible, women, and apples. Eating apples, thus making them a national food, means assuming the burden of enlightening the world while siding with the serpent. Who can frighten a people whom the devil and the serpent respect? Don't they meet the qualifications to be a metropolis? And what role rightfully belongs to a metropolis if not to dust off History and put it back in its true perspective?

Is feudalism really dead? Or have the limits and enclosures just changed? From this vantage point, you see people moving around in blocks with little flags planted in front of each fortress. From time to time there are attempted surprise attacks, as if to test the enemy's readiness. And all around the ballet masters you see urchins dancing, happy to play with the paper streamers tossed to them: a real aviary full of roosters, some of them castrated but still touchy and hopping mad! All feed on the strength of the giants in whose shadow they shrink. It's understandable why America sometimes has fits of pique when children walk over her flower beds; not to have been able to acquire good manners during the time spent under her tutelage implies the most flagrant ill will. One Way! Guardian of the peace, America often launches fireworks to enlighten, dazzle, and reassure the whole world. Deep down she wants to allow a swarm of liberties to pollinate every land: if it so happens that she supplies arms, that's just to support the flowering of freedom.

Having always basked in such an ambience, Americans welcome you in their homes, heart in hand; then, at the end of the visit, they leave you at the door, where their domain and territorial waters end. They close the door on your heels with a smiling good-bye, their hands waving in such a way that you want to turn around. At this point, you can get stuck in the elevator or wander in endless corridors—that's up to you. Isn't it true that America gives every person the exceptional opportunity to succeed or get lost? Now firmly established, the first arrivals produce for the new immigrants looking for land, and, in the supermarkets of the former, the latter find everything to continue their journey. Thus, the great transhumance noticeable on land and in air is explainable in this nation eager to transport entire trains by ferry in order to save time. To maintain the pioneer tradition, cultivate the memory of these valiant knights, children are still told stories of pirates and buccaneers. Specialized magazines publish pictures of women followed and captured by pirates. That seems a wonder in this civilization where women seem to rule. Everyone agrees to this homage, even the victim who considers herself honored by the exceptional treatment she's forced to suffer. In the labs of Mr. American, men prepare themselves angrily for the competition. They eat Energez, Enertol, Hi-Protein, Super-Protein, Bon-Gro, muscle makers in less than ten weeks. The new muscle-bound American is soon going to get up on the stage and, with a flick, sweep away all the runts who persist in measuring only two feet. For now, liberated women sit in the saddle, eyes blazing, staring at the eye of a camera, ready to carry to the ends of the earth, as a masterpiece, the image of their nude body—up-to-date women playing with dolls and toy lions...

*

* *

For the security of working populations in a world not yet purged of its primitive instincts, the government maintains hordes and hordes of servicemen, whose number it, perhaps, doesn't even know. And these servicemen, just as all those from other continents, make great strides to get closer to the war that recedes from them. Falling at random, the shells they fire in emergencies leave their hands clean and their consciences free; it's not their fault if war had the gall to flee the battlefield and take refuge in cities. As disarmed as the civilians, it seeks refuge among them! Executioners and sadists are the ones who kill up close in order to witness the mortal agony of their enemy. With today's new intelligent weapons, war is joyous and death anonymous. You never know who fired. It's an absolute joy to see a high-ranking American serviceman walk. At the threshold of a doorway he stops for a bit, raises his nose, hesitates a bit, to fool the enemy about his direction, and then is ready to be first to move. Could he be superstitious? He measures his steps, studies their comings and goings as he would for a shooting, then, resolute, decisive, he leaves—calm, solid, straight. A modern knight, he knows what he represents. The gold bars on his shoulders show even more clearly the importance of his role and position in a society that can dance and make love because he's watching over the frontiers of the empire. His foot is not an automatic foot but a foot which reasons and can cross all slopes. A man unable to be surprised except in rare moments of relaxation, of letting go, at the precise moment he brings a cigarette to his mouth and takes out the lighter. In this bit of time he holds himself aloof from his group, his team, his unit, his corps, becoming a man again, capable of deploring the horrors of war he is required to prepare and have carried out by the people. He also suffers discipline. This man never attacks; his weapons aren't those that scratch and spare; they're otherworldly weapons, delivered by people who never have the time to bypass an obstacle. New spirits that swoop down on you from the depths of the earth, from underneath the oceans and the clouds; new masters of thunder and lightning, at whose sight the world trembles from limb to limb.

Such a frightening country makes an unheard-of effort to put a little black blood into the veins of her government; she hugs the blacks so closely that they'd all be dead if they weren't Americans. She'd hug them to the point of smothering them in order to save her milk supply; for the crux of the problem is the precious milk supply, which blacks risk exhausting without even succeeding in becoming white, except, perhaps for their nails. Women redden their lips and relax their hair but not under the influence of milk. To have drunk American milk for centuries and remained black is a phenomenon which no one can explain. It can only come from the malice of a devil not yet evolved since the dawn of time. Although hand in glove with the serpent for the marketing of the apple which he can't do without, Americans are deeply religious. The black is either a devil or a ghost, but if he were a devil, he'd speak another dialect than American. So he must be a ghost. And who isn't afraid of ghosts? Who doesn't fight them? But where do all these light-skinned blacks come from? The sun? weather? or a product other than milk? Or maybe a black woman was taken by some white without the blacks objecting in the least. Would this color have enough self-confidence to confront all the others?

Fear of blacks ensues from an old story, so old that very few people remember it. This country, which catches fire very easily because of her ardent fervor, experienced several fires which were attributed to blacks since they alone could profit from burning the fields and houses of their guardians. Such audacity couldn't go unpunished. Thirty blacks were burned alive as an example. So that no one in the world could protest, three whites, picked up who knows where, were included.[48] This new type of equality, established in the shadow of Liberty, was necessary: one white is worth ten blacks. It's not yet known what the white American woman is worth in relation to the black American woman. We'll know one day because America can't stand ambiguity. And because the black American woman isn't yet situated, her whole race is relegated to the periphery of cities, or is made into cores or belts for other ones that are past masters in the art of judo. Many cities wear black belts which are slowly climbing up their body; a minority outside the walls, praying to a suburban god, a god of places where water can freely stagnate after rains; sentinels guarding the sleep of those whose epic history is taught in every school of the nation; black shadows destined to sustain the brilliance of the other states' colors; powerful men, chrysalises waiting for the molting hour to enter the large white family of New World bosses; ladders leading to Africa, ladders long scorned whose importance has been rediscovered. Although Americans, blacks bear the weight of the anathema men cast on their country of origin. Every black in every country has lived through the same experience; and many, in their confusion, have tried to barter their color for the model white color, even though their baptisms never allowed them to penetrate the boss's fortress. Many are those who look at them from the perspective[49] of their own interests. Abel and Cain worshiped the same god; blacks and whites who have the same first name, the same patron saint, pray to the same god but in their respective neighborhoods. Here, you see, there are separate, second-class gods. But what can be done when prayers don't focus on the same

48. At the beginning of the War for Independence. The Robert Gould Shaw and 54th Regiment Memorial at Beacon and Park streets in Boston commemorates the event.

49. Dadié used the word *yeux* in quotes, translated here as *perspective* instead of the literal *eyes*. Here I do not maintain Dadié's quotes.

goals? Separating the churches already classifies the petitions, facilitating the work of the angels who, in turn, throw them into a production line that allows an intense profitability. Angels also work in shifts to collect every prayer that men say every minute.

Given their proud bearing, servicemen don't always attract sympathy, and this proves that the American people simply put up with the army. Michigan students, who let themselves be easily crushed by their Nebraska friends, refuse the same honor to the West Point cadets. The unarmed cadets stood up and sat down in unison but didn't succeed in gathering their wits, despite their uniforms and regulation haircuts. The spectators didn't do anything to help them either. To the contrary! Their civic spirit won out over their warlike instinct. But a national army could not lose face, and eighty officers led a cannon onto the field in order to bring their flock back in line. The sight of the cannon on such a cramped field still didn't stir up the courage of the West Point cadets. Instead it annoyed the "Michiganers." You should have seen those Michiganers! They came unglued at the sight of this cannon, its little deadly mouth pointed toward their parents, friends, and girlfriends! They ran up and down; they huddled together; they were determined to fight an army supposed to be invincible. West Point was giving way, the crowd applauding and yelling their heads off. Children screamed: Michigan! Women yelled: Michigan! Men threw their hats in the air, jumping for joy to catch them. Finally, the army was going to be liquidated, eliminated from the budget. Ouch! And this honor would go to Michigan, which had the courage of its convictions.

West Point was losing. A blank cannon shot was fired while a plane flew over the field, filling the sky with the noise of its motor as if to drown out the crowds. This whole drama was necessary to give back a soul to the soldiers. With this boost, they scored a goal. Nevertheless, the cannon couldn't continue to fire and Michigan won. Finally the national anthem was sung to reconcile the people of a nation almost divided by an ordinary football game. The army left with dignity to the applause of the Michiganers who had found their team spirit along with the other stars of the banner. There's the proof—the West Point cadets have shown it: the American is not a cloak-and-dagger hero. When you eat cold foods, drink very cold drinks, and munch ice cubes all day long, how can you have enough warm blood rising to your head that you can pick a quarrel with someone? Why the hordes of soldiers covering land and sea? Why train men to live permanently in air and under water, in steel boxes that the elements sometimes crush with a flick? All these people join the army for the free trips, the desirable work, the combat, the risks. Everyone joins because they love to fight, or they want to obey government orders placed on billboards in fashionable neighborhoods: "Make yourself seen by the world!" America is so far away that her existence is sometimes in doubt; so it's up to her to prove that she exists and can be reckoned with. "Make yourself seen by friends and enemies. Reassure the former, discourage the latter." People enlist in the army's empire to become pioneers, conquerors of lands, hearts, and markets. Everyone must know that America, continent of immense potential, produces commodities for immediate consumption: vegetables, citrus fruits, meat, clothing, drinks for men, men for machines and cannons, new bosses for the world. In this country, where there's a tendency to put everything within the reach of the individual, who is fast becoming a king served by machines, you're constantly given the impression that Americans are still wondering what to put at the top of their list of values: business, machines, or men. Sworn to commit suicide if they don't succeed in rating man first, American citizens wear a necktie, just in case. Since John Brown was hanged for trying to place all Americans on the same level, it can't honestly be said that other Americans have committed suicide either for whites or for blacks. No matter! Everyone wears a necktie, reassuring us of their good intentions. And if, in international assemblies, no one forces the issues, it's for fear of having American cadavers to deal with. It's true that an American cadaver is not to be buried hastily, so true, in fact, that the respect accorded human beings has been extended to include machines, notably American cars, whose cadavers always sit in state royally among other vehicular carcasses. Americans need to be surrounded.

But where, when, and how will this vertigo sweeping the country end? Is all that noise deliberately produced to distract shrewd tourists? Is this oceanic roar that New York unleashes night and day the sound of future cities, where men would only be bobbing corks? What volcano is brooding under this continent where everyone wants to wear a smile? Does the huge tarantula spin its web across the world to survive or because of bulimia? Whatever the answer may be, America will need to rethink the problem of man, who came to the new continent to live in the shadow of Liberty.

*

* *

Americans like to teach others even if, inspired by the profit motive, they up their prices at the same time. So toothbrush and towel in hand, they'll show you how to brush your teeth and dry off after a bath. Evidently, American water has special virtues to which not every brush in the world is accustomed. They don't have bad intentions, just charitable concern about fitting foreigners with the American measuring tape and plumb line.

By pushing the notion of savings and effort to the extreme, speakers barely open their mouths while talking. Words themselves instinctively contract and become a whisper. Consequently, an American, calm by nature, will remain silent in a car, letting the radio talk, which, like television, is neither frosty nor mute. This man who is of so few words that women avoid him, comes into his own as soon as a meeting begins: each person speaks calmly, embellishing his remarks with "OKs," and "goods," followed closely by an "also," which requires an "in brief," which emphasizes nothing. The speaker is only at the colon in a new paragraph. The American sentence takes long, supple strides—lionlike.

It no longer surprises me that these perpetually rushed people yell a brief "hello" in passing since, one cold morning, I saw one, face purple, belching forth smoke from mouth and nostrils. It's the sacred fire burning in him, the same fire flowing in forges and foundries. The machine is transparent in the smallest gesture: an arm becomes a piston, a leg a crank arm, the person a crank. Factory assembly lines fetter citizens, who no longer have time to run to the barber, the grocer, the pharmacist, the restaurateur, or the bookseller. The drugstore, reconstituting early family life, opens its doors to them. A more agglutinated cell is giving birth to a new race of men.

How can anyone ask American machines to get in step when they have to dress a new human generation getting taller and taller all the time? In this insane race toward gigantism, women still have some common sense, some moderation. Hotel managers could be pulling out their hair in frustration since they never know how tall the client who books a room is. But no—because they've more than one string in their bow, they keep a full head of hair and their clients always leave delighted. What else but extension beds? America thinks of everything and has a solution for everything—she is the new village sorceress!

*

* *

American craftiness has no equal, except for that of a Dioula[50] trader. A man can talk to you, while, at the same time, check out the other shoppers and weigh the pound of onions someone is buying. The citizen of this powerful nation feels you out without you even knowing it, and he does so with the friendliest of smiles. It's not in his character to wound a soul, a heart, a man. If there are in this country oil barons, it's only to make sure each gear in the social, economic, and political life gets its drop of lubricant. To run as silently as a new motor is one of America's strengths. Therefore, there aren't many offices where people call out to each other or move around to chat. After all, aren't there telephones to shorten distances and make "offices" humming beehives?

And so it was that one day the president of a large university greeted a group of foreign students who had come to be initiated into the mysteries of the American dialect. Long speeches interrupted by much applause. No longer knowing what to do with their hands since subjugating machines, Americans spend their time applauding and being applauded. Any other than American hands would be covered with blisters from hailing speakers on all sides: the most sensitive part of the body is the hand, and it shouldn't be given to just anyone.

After a two-week "intensive course," tests verified that the students could follow the speech of a very old president without getting lost. And he spoke a long time. I didn't understand a single word of his speech, but my beaming face, my enthusiastic clapping, and rapt attention—indeed, my whole bearing—testified that I had followed the eloquent and profound address perfectly. I was still clapping when the others stopped, worn out. Several spunky ones tried to keep up but quickly admitted defeat. I took the clapping prize by sheer force. That gave me class and, in any other country but America, would have made me a person of considerable prestige, one whose most casual opinions could be influential. Here, everyone only stared at me. I kept on clapping and could have continued, making everyone dance, if my neighbor hadn't elbowed me out of my ecstasy. These people—they don't even let you dream!

— He's a good speaker...
— Yes.
— Did you understand?
— Yes.

50. The dispersed Muslim long-distance traders of West Africa, Dioula traders were noted as gold traders and skilled craftsmen and are still active in commercial life.

—What did you think about his speech?
—Please?
—Did you like it?
—Yes.

Finally the time came... The guests rose. I followed suit... Ooof! Happy at last to escape as fast as possible my talkative friend, who had exhausted my supply of English in only a few minutes. He looked as if he might follow me: I plunged even deeper into the crowd, straight ahead. Alas, my adventures were only beginning. I followed the others into a room where we had to line up for a receiving line of young ladies. Who was being chosen in this beauty contest—them or us? It was not a beauty contest after all: the girls gave us tags on which we had to write our name and nationality—bow ties to attach to our coat lapel. Another line for us to go greet and thank the honorable president and his party was awaiting our respects in another room. A long line, slow, plodding, like those you see in front of theaters. I now understand why American shoes have double soles; they're worn out standing in line, the only real opportunity here to have feet on the ground, touching the earth. No one complains. They could stand there in the bitterest cold for hours on end—it makes you tough! The good president extended his hand and asked me several questions. For me, he rearranged the questions, so there I was in distress, utterly lost in the "was," the "don'ts," the "did," the "I'm," the "U" pronounced "A," the "O" pretending to be "A." I was drowning. The good man, pulling me toward him, leaned closer, like a kindly grandfather, and helped me build and pull out my sentences. My poor ill-matched baby sentences, frightened by so many people, were sticking in my gut. I was making a terrific effort to give birth, but a cord stubbornly held them back. He understood that I was about to blush. Clearly, the fact that my hair was standing on end signaled the approach of this marvel to behold. Unwilling to take on this strange and scandalous phenomenon, he kindly passed me on to his wife, who was satisfied to ask me my "first name." I knew it by heart, at least this "first name" preceding the one I received the day when, cleansed of original sin, I was admitted, in principle, to the company of the true sons of God. Everyone was expecting Him to perform a miracle He dared not perform—changing my color—so I was held at arm's length, waiting for Him to decide my case and that of all my people. The white God can't figure out how to adopt His dark sons who are dying of cold on the threshold of His kingdom.

Being very political or having a highly developed maternal instinct, the president's wife didn't push her husband's investigation any further, refraining from asking even the eternal "where are you from?" I then approached a young man. His lack of experience with human weaknesses, his youthful irritability, not yet civilized by setbacks, caused him to blow right in my face: "How are you?" In that hot, dry wind, I managed a quick: "Thank you." It was only a sentence fragment, but it allowed me to be weighed, judged, and condemned in the mind of that speaker: he dropped my hand the way one drops the hand of someone who refuses to be helped, to be saved. Off you go! To be spared from these interrogators, I was going to lose myself in the buzzing crowd when a girl handed me a quarter of a glass of fruit juice, artificial of course. It wasn't exactly the right moment to confess to her that, since my arrival, I'd been throwing up all the sweets I'd been stuffed with. She wouldn't understand. At best she would ask herself countless questions about the qualities and capacity of the black stomach, an excellent subject for a Ph.D. dissertation. I was admiring those Japanese women, glancing at their smooth, unsmiling faces; no matter where they are, they come equipped with their safety belts, the mainstay of their national costume, an elementary precaution when one is from an island. A beautiful brunette motioned to me while I was looking for a place to get rid of my white elephant of a glass. More questions? Had she discerned in my expression the anxiety that still afflicted me? Had I actually blushed? No mirror on the wall to check. At her second sign, I went over. She was going to teach me to pronounce the English "th." I had to give her credit. She was a masterpiece of American organization—a true human factory! She inserted her tongue between her teeth and patiently repeated a word I'd never heard. Tongue between teeth, she rounded the roughness, leveled the ruggedness, filled in the chasms, and knocked down the peaks of the language whose charm I was beginning to discover. She closed her eyes as if to better appreciate the flavor of the English "th": seeing her carried away, I wondered why the whole world wasn't speaking English. I was becoming aware of my backwardness, that I had, for over a quarter-century, been living outside a very important circuit. Another universe was opening up before me, one I had to fit in order to be complete. Obviously no one had ever taught me to speak English, had ever given me the opportunity to pronounce the "th."

As he was leaving, the president passed us, smiled, and made a gesture to comfort me and encourage me to learn his beautiful language.

The young man who had dropped my hand like a hot potato was dancing—scornfully, proudly, his tall frame defying time, a young American who would need a lot of experience to conquer the world. He was like some people who can't win the hearts of others because they themselves lack heart. I don't think the worthy president took away a favorable impression of the drawing power of his language. Between two English "th's," the lady and I were using the silky language of Paris to communicate. A wise old man, he understood perfectly how difficult it is to cope with a jumble of sounds that are written without being pronounced or pronounced without being written. Nor did he forget all those sounds that are to be swallowed, chewed, whistled, or that need the throat for volume, weight, and amplitude, not to mention the numerous and disconcerting nasal sounds. The old president also knew that his country is the only one in the world to welcome travelers in the glow of Liberty. Though the most sordid dictatorships swoop down on the continent, no one can deny that America is the country of Liberty. The lady appears on stamps, postcards, screens, and books. She constitutes one of the country's principal resources. Liberty is an American property; no nation could take this seal of quality away from her. Paris could speak of her statue at the Grenelle Bridge, but it is an atrophied Liberty that doesn't seem to measure up to New York's lavish and provocative one—a true Liberty. The torch can be trimmed in order to make the flame itself brighter, but Liberty can't be taken from her island, guarded as she is by a battalion of skyscrapers. On her screens America, perhaps purposely, exhibits the Empire State Building and the Statue of Liberty as the two essential monuments of the continent, showing what Liberty has allowed her to build. For now, other states have only seen and imported buildings. But, obviously, having monuments to the dead and tombs of the unknown soldier implies that they are partisans of Liberty who know how to sacrifice joyously for her.

Before ending our pronunciation session, the beautiful Americanized Mexican lady gave me her address and phone number, courteously following rules of hospitality.

You can call me when you like, or come to my house, but call me first. Bye! You must learn to speak English. I'll help you. You can do it!—Bye!

How easy it is to win over Americans! All you have to do is not be able to pronounce their "th." I suspect America's still looking for allies against her former colonizer by making them stumble over the famous "th" and thus demonstrate how difficult the English mentality is. I thought the Mexican lady was going to turn around and say another "bye," but she had hung up; I was no longer on her line. She lost herself in the crowd and I, in the meanderings of questions that neighbors began to ask me. She had left, the one who had saved me from blushing, from scandalizing everyone, from working every scholar in the universe to death. Thanks to her I could remain black. And most important of all, I could call her. So I slept, the sweet song of the English "th" in my ear. The next morning, I dialed the number: the telephone rang once, twice. Before the third ring, someone picked up the receiver, a voice that no longer put its tongue between the teeth to pronounce the "th" but rolled it, brandishing it like a club. What had become of the sweet, charming, enchanting "th" of the evening before? Was this an unreliable, rough language, just now showing its true face? Or do American women experience so much resentment and anger the day after an English lesson that they roar like a wounded panther?

There are people who maintain that America is leased out, that it's really private property. In whose hands? the ogre's or the siren's, whose voice breathes so much charm into the harsh English dialect? We should say "unleashed," so "unleashed," in fact, I'd like to see all Americans smoking a pipe.[51] They have such a beautiful way of smoking, of making halos of those swirling clouds! It's not surprising that tobacco would find a paradise here. Smoke seems to be able to spread out only on this vast continent, where it can freely go wherever it pleases. All the factories of this monster United States of America, whose shape is frightening, participate in this strategy of covering up. Often blocking the sky, factory smoke doesn't always allow good views and doesn't allow sufficient vision for men accustomed to counting in blocks of houses to better emphasize the community spirit that is their goal. Side by side like blocks of houses, these men can, nevertheless, stop to pick you up in their car because a taxi didn't hear you call or signal. They're now opening up to other cultures. In fact, they're blooming. Americans, who seem to live in order to produce gold, accumulate wealth, save money to travel, and run from one continent to another, have a complex and, as revenge, don't like to see anyone lounging about. This term doubtless

51. Dadié plays on the words *affermé* ('strengthened') and *affermie* ('leased'). I translated the former as *unleashed* to convey the idea of strength and retain the word similarity.

doesn't even exist in the language. Even the men I've seen window-shopping look like generals inspecting their troops.

As soon as you set foot in a store or post office someone looks up or runs over to ask: "May I help you?" He's always mobilized to aid, help, and soothe. He wants to make sure his company is pleasant and your stay profitable, for people come to America to get rich. No one leaves this country without taking something away, without leaving something of himself: to get rich is an exchange. Several people seem to have seen in Americans only teeth inherited from the English. But how could teeth raised on fortified milk fail to get larger and fatter? Rest assured, though, that even when an American shows them in anger, he knows they're hardly aggressive, just baby teeth. As the whole world knows, America protects herself with planes, boats, and other death devices in order to pass off baby teeth as wisdom teeth. When Americans appear in this gear, frightened people offer thousands of compliments about America's lofty ideas, her magnanimousness, her clear understanding of the world's problems, her delicate taste and dazzling intelligence—in short, babbling everything you would, in a similar circumstance, to save your soul, tell a robber who waylays you in a dark alley. Americans are no fools. They know their friends mock their baby teeth and their casual way of approaching serious matters. Everything here is a sport, a contest—competition: this is the essential character of America, competition among men, buildings, and companies! Who'll get there first?

People here drink enormous quantities of milk because they don't have time to watch a dish stew slowly and cook it to a turn, with all the natural flavors collected by wind, smoke, and sun. Thanks to special cookbooks, everyone in America knows that a chicken is done in fifteen minutes. The books say that chicken is cooked in fifteen minutes, so it is, even if it's raw: there are pots trained to whistle to tell you so: "Come and get your chicken, it's ready." At the signal, there they are, dashing toward the machine to congratulate it. It could have eaten the chicken, but you open its stomach to rescue the dish.

American women have succeeded in relegating men to the kitchen, where they're very proud of their white hats, which at least distinguish them from the women. Being lazy, they defer meal preparation to machines, but even American machines don't yet have a tongue. The customers in restaurants have to finish the preparation of a dish themselves. They'd never eat without the bottles with bizarre names on the table at their fingertips. It's the only way to ensure quality control for food and collaborate in its preparation. Even in this empire of the mechanical, the final step of mixing the food takes place in the stomach. From time to time, though, people have their revenge and can impose their presence, as if they refuse to be mere playthings or fodder for machines. All their dreams revolt in an effort to seize ascendancy from their robots. Universities fight constantly against the machine, by putting students on domestic jobs: serving and cleaning tables, washing and ironing laundry, washing dishes. In this country stuffed with gold, where everything is allowed, students learn to serve before demanding to be served. Professors are the first to set an example, standing in line to choose and take the plate they want; and, just like students, they return their trays—democratic America survives in the universities. Is that why some refuse contact with other colors? Americans can now be understood when certain childish vanities seem monstrous to them: they can't understand what strange phenomenon pushes a poor country to pretend to be rich.

* * *

A mad terror buffets the country seasonally. Everyone sits up straight, yelling at the Tartar standing up at the edge of his territorial waters. Wise men speak; and friends who can barely stand on their own two feet send messages, mobilizing troops to show the quality of their vassalage. They make an infernal racket around the suzerain as if there'd been an eclipse. The newspapers feed the warlike fires, and television shows an hysterical parade of highly developed death machines, applauded by roused crowds for whom death takes on the joyous colors of life.[52] They doubtless think that the death of a man in another country lengthens the time of their own existence.

People probably become more narrow-minded, limited, and chauvinistic the more their homes try to reach the stars. Houses certainly have windows, through which the other buildings, modern anthills, can be watched. An anthill is only a building imagined and built by ants: we're all becoming ant-peoples. Thus, the tension slowly climbs, oscillates, settles in. Everyone prepares his weapons: women prepare their black veils, men brush their war uniforms, and children study old portraits of heroes in books and think of those they must again take as a role model. The eleventh hour! They wait for the shock, the cataclysm, the fire—in

52. Dadié is referring to the 1963 Cuban missile crisis.

a day, three hours, a minute, two seconds... Everyone's on edge, hanging on a few words, a bit of hope, a sudden burst of human intelligence, a beneficial miscalculation, a revolt of Life—a categorical No! shouted from all the lungs in the world, frightening the blood merchants, dream doctors, and dealers of every stripe—green flies buzzing around cradles and living rooms. Then the fever slowly ebbs, falls, disappears. The world is saved! America, where machines on toll bridges catch queue jumpers, can pursue her path, that is, continue to eat by candlelight, to see more clearly in semidarkness. Again, vassals acclaim the great power, and after having banished the devil, Adam, and Eve from Eden, have some refreshments and rest by the glow of candlelight.

By making us aware of our progress, the use of candles links us to the past and reduces our pride. What poetry and lessons in the naked, frightened flame with which the wind toys! To eat, argue, and make love by such light is to try to have your feet on the ground. Even on the thirtieth floor, Americans will light a candle to keep their feet on the ground, that is, to remind them that there're still people in the world who can do without the necessities, who can sleep under the stars, surrounded by insects. But that doesn't prevent them from believing that people are better housed and clothed, that they are warmer if they grow up white. This is an old kind of thinking that Americans have taken on with them on their exodus and planted so well in certain states that citizens carry its logic to the extreme, decreeing that day and night can't possibly sit at the same table or in the same park. Does day fear that night will claim her stars?

The practice of dining by candlelight, dancing, and flirting is most pronounced in young people, who follow a millennial tradition to the letter. When they plan a party, the first thing they think of is an adequate supply of candles, then Coca-Cola and straws to drink it, and finally sweets. All this is supposed to help them read into the heart and eyes of their friends, unless, of course, the dim light reflects the color and intensity of their own feelings—vague and vacillating. Here dating takes on its full meaning and importance: no one can blame a savvy American girl for playing hard to get when dealing with guys who talk about their ardent passion by the dying candlelight. In her place, who wouldn't be skeptical?

Adopting a frightened lost-dog look, she is cautious, jumps as soon as you approach to catch her breath, her hand on her heart to keep it from sinking. Does your question seem difficult? She is "I'm sorry," then consults her watch to see how many minutes have been wasted uselessly and goes on her way, head held high. She puts her finger on the American's reason for being: not to be late. Late, but he is late, has been for centuries and millennia! What time is he trying to make up in his infernal race? He claims time is money, so there he is, greedily shouting himself hoarse just to chase it in a most cruel run for the money. Here, there, and everywhere linger the bones of time; in butcher shops hang filets of time; at the deli sizzle twists of time; in the banks sleep ingots of time; and in ladies' purses suffocate honeycombs of time. Time—there's the enemy of modern man.

The most obvious symptoms of America's lateness are her Guinness-like superlatives—the world's tallest building, the fastest airplane, the whitest house, the first lady, the largest statue. In their pursuit of time, Americans cut and grind it up faster than Europeans, and thus have become a mere shadow of what they could've been. In their infernal race for supremacy, they've discarded and forgotten the principles which precipitated the break with the old country—unless of course, they had intended to make the new continent a workshop to produce arms for a reconquest. So be it. America, a botched Europe, is a country hanging on between two continents. A flashy fleet allows her to weather storms and daze competitors, but what of the masses who support the weight of the tempest-defying skyscrapers? Was it for such a heaven that the *Jesus,* Hawkins's ship, transported blacks from their African hell? Some people say that America should change, but what can America change in the giant network which allows her to float toward mastery of the world? What stumbling blocks must she avoid in her triumphant march? Meanwhile, let's just hope that the earth doesn't one day collapse under the footsteps of this modern giant.

The ancient Gauls were only afraid that the sky might fall; the Americans are afraid of being caught between heaven and earth, both in rebellion.

*
* *

One look at the population figures of America would suggest that machines help in reproduction. However, the truth is that the American dead remain on earth because they receive nothing for crossing over the river. Americans—such practical people—wonder why they have to give money to a failure, to someone who's stopped the assembly line by agreeing to die. But what river would he cross where there wasn't a bridge? Even dead, Americans remain geniuses, engineers who can erect the most marvelous bridges on all the rivers of the universe. The country's dead leave, thus, empty-handed, sometimes without even having lived, their passion having been to accumulate the most gold possible. Life for some has been a game of checkers, consisting of sweeping off the most pieces from the opponent; seen from another perspective, a game of chess. Saint Peter already knows them: they introduce themselves with pockets full of plans for hide-a-beds and sofa-tables—undoubtedly conceived under the seal of the devil.

The Russians pose no fundamental problem with their red flag: they're people with one idea, one goal, one color. They call attention to themselves from a distance, while the Americans—all blues, reds, whites, and stars—present embarrassing problems of color and of precedence. As for black Americans—they're no longer particularly interesting, since American whites pulled off the miraculous coup of making Redskins of them, persuading them to wear feathers in their hats. So much wiliness and spitefulness makes Saint Peter very suspicious, but Americans are past masters in the art of camouflage. In this country—where Standard Oil crushes churches with the weight of all its oil, concrete, and scrap iron, where people pray God to grant that they not die under the debris of twenty immense floodgates of oil—it's said that men often leave for Heaven, undone by forgetting to pick a number before lining up.

Numerous multiracial enemies spin out some very instructive, albeit embellished, yarns for a study of the American character.

Once upon a time in Paradise, the American saints were bored to death. They longed for a death that wouldn't come. Their customary habits having been upset, they missed the earth, where they were bosses. Several had asked to go to Hell, but the decision was fixed. No opportunity for sin. One morning, one American took out from who knows where a cash register. Right away all the American saints lined up to pay for what they were using in Paradise.

—What's going on? said Saint Peter, rushing up.

—Well, we're paying for what we eat.

—But here it's Paradise... everything is free...

—Where we come from, only getting into museums is free.

—Please... we're in Paradise. Everything here is held communally...

—Haven't we made a mistake coming here to enemy territory? We prefer to return to earth.

— But you've chosen Paradise.
— We didn't know what it was like.

Since then, Saint Peter is supposed to have refused them admittance, not because they're Protestants by birth but because of their membership in the mole family, because they're forever digging canals, tunnels, and galleries. Can you imagine how a Paradise occupied by Americans would look? One Ways here, One Ways there, elsewhere banks, factories, and buildings connected by tiered bridges. At sunset that fiendish, lustful dance called the twist, not to mention that paradise could become a summer residence for American millionaires! Unbeknownst to Americans, who continue to keep the Bible at their bedside in order to become fishers of men, Saint Peter finds them too yellow.[53]

The Bible-in-one-hand-and-sword-in-the-other style is passé. Men are regaining control of their own time while America seems to want all watches set by her time so she won't have to change hers. We must assume that this country draws others into her orbit to better stifle them: they'll die suffocated or seized with vertigo because no one can build a taller building, at least with America watching. In the tunnels of their buildings they become rigid and in their shadows they're dying from lack of sun. A terrible dilemma! And so, to give time for reflection, hotels hang out "Do Not Disturb" signs on doorknobs, because America keeps thinking about what she has to do to prepare the way for tomorrow's world, which she has harnessed to her own chariot. She plans to simplify everything in order to give man back his original freedom, that is, harness him to only one chariot. Not yet steel, the American heart gushes love, a love which is often misunderstood since it's measured in inches and feet. No one knows what abyss the American foot can dig or how much atmospheric pressure the inch can cause—discordant elements confirmed by America's will to free men from all metrical slavery, all iron, ice, butter, and gold dynasties. She wants to suppress the middlemen—better yet, gobble them up. The world will only find peace and quiet again in the American belly, in the empire of business, invigorated by tumultuous rivers of golden blood. Copper and cobalt give her insomnia and increase her strength. The excess of her vitality is to be shared with friendly partners and subjects.

53. Dadié uses the term "jaunes" to mean scabs, strikebreakers. The translation remains "yellow" to imply deceitfulness.

She wants to become the vital inspiration of our era and direct the ballet that is man's daily existence with more dexterity, audacity, and mastery. It's understandable why Americans shrink from their dead. For them death is so intimately associated with life that it can't exist apart from it. Death is the static aspect of existence, a form of life that wouldn't be welcomed in a country where everything exudes the joy of living. This joy of living is so ensconced in people's hearts that hospitals have nice little stores, even cafeterias, where visitors can refresh themselves before going into the sickrooms. Walls are painted in bright colors and nurses are dressed in blue, pink, and white. When relatives and friends come out, saddened by the sight of those suffering, they're immediately thrown into motion, joy sweeping them into the dynamic flow of life. Right away they forget what they could have seen as suffering. They dissociate themselves from the negative side of life, and follow their path with even more true grit, swearing to triumph over every handicap.

Americans stride along, heroically tracing the steps of Columbus who, in order to save a suffocating Europe, linked two continents. His discovery didn't cause universal joy—far from it. I doubt, for example, that the Redskins celebrate the fateful day they met the West. To comprehend what a giant step America has taken since Columbus planted the cross and abandoned it for gold and gems, please count the number of buildings erected, cans of corned-beef hawked, cannons cast, warships built, and on and on. But no one dares tackle this tiresome task, cynical about the proven brutality of America's production capacity. For some time now America has outgrown the cowboy stage to enter a more refined phase. No one in the world excuses himself before foreigners as much as an American, fully aware of protocol. Push him and he will be the first to excuse himself for taking too much space, for forgetting the rules of hospitality. Americans have created wide sidewalks for people to feel at ease, for they insist that tourists, once here, across the border, feel at home. Everyone will make that effort as soon as you are in their particular circle. Taken carefully in hand, your feet won't touch the earth for a while; then, one morning, they'll drop you, but by then you'll have sprouted wings for your own flight. Every telephone call will injure your pride because the caller will tell you, almost always, without ever having seen you: "Yes, Claude; I'm sorry, Emmanuel; goodbye John." This friendly way of treating tourists is one of America's great charms. Isn't the telephone made to bring people together, to connect them? And isn't that why you find one in every bedroom? in hotel lobbies? in public places? in the street? What would this immense country be without the telephone? What a marvel of perfection and rapid communication, when the line isn't busy! In several minutes you can reach a city located hundreds of kilometers away. The music of the phone amuses Americans so much that they spend most of their time attached to this fantastic toy, this new tam-tam which keeps him in the production line. What would modern America be without the "jet" and the telephone?

*

* *

Ah, if I were Parisian, what a statue I would have had erected for grateful America! After all, doesn't she show one of the most important children of my country in a particularly exceptional light? The strange man who preferred the poor man's hearse to that of the powerful with whom he truly belonged? Today, people still don't understand him. Because he played with lightning and left sparks in his trail, they consider him "outmoded." But they're the ones who haven't yet matured enough to grasp the importance of his message. He remains contemporary because even in our era all the John Browns and their friends are still hanging. To hasten black integration into the larger family, to suppress all social inequalities, the ideas of Victor Hugo are updated so as to make them more digestible, more easily understood. Under the new packaging, readers can now savor them, grasp them, understand them. Americans have bottled them—as a liqueur. Oh yes, America has given the name Victor Hugo to a type of brandy as heady as the poems of this immortal writer—a very clever, modern way of allowing men to absorb and, above all, appreciate the ideas of brotherhood and equality championed by this writer. If they lack the time to read them, people can drink them. "Good idea." Hugo produces dividends, gold. In him, Paris will have lost everything except honor.

Smacking their lips, these American cannibals savor one of the best sons of Paris, one of the greatest poets of the world; yes, these builders of cubes, cones, and trapezoids even drink Hugo from the bottle in order better to incorporate his gray matter. For Paris to be eaten, read, or drunk by Americans always means holding high the torch of Liberty; and all things considered, it's better to be in the American belly than in any other. It makes Parisian meat even more appreciated. Hugo! If only he hadn't turned the Americans against him with his story of John

Brown![54] Why did he have to get involved in this murky business anyway? How can they be blamed for drinking him, not having been able to munch him? This is further proof of their understanding. This is the most obvious sign of their progress—drinking the blood and ideas of the enemy.

The example of Victor Hugo has been so profitable that they systematically bleed all the famous men of Paris. An important branch of the Parisian dynasty, the Bourbons, have also been bottled in this country, where everything must be channeled. Whiskey. Many in this country are still royalists at heart and love to go to fancy dinners.

The conflicts that can break out between New York and Paris have obscure origins in this American obsession to shamelessly profit from great Parisian names. The national wound festers and sometimes inflames dialogues, which very quickly turn into monologues. Certain foreign speeches are so clearly affected that Americans chew them over before absorbing them. Even speeches by their great men receive the same treatment. They're listened to with open mouths, then chewed, and finally brooded over in order for the flavor and impact to be better grasped. This habit's said to have come from the milk virus[55] which they haven't yet succeeded in tracking down. How can people who constantly brood over ideas whose color is never seen be trusted? Americans suffer greatly from this detestable disease, which doesn't always allow them the victories expected in international meetings, since everyone is wary of them. Therefore, they've readied all their researchers for action, giving them the express mission of locating this famous milk virus. Do you think that they stopped drinking milk because of that? They drank it yesterday and they'll drink it tomorrow, virus or no virus. And when it's found, they'll certainly drink it, for to act otherwise wouldn't be in good taste. Like a soldier mobilized on all fronts, from production to the rational consumption of time, no one will fail in this mission. Each citizen will fight to the end in order for the machine to keep moving.

In this business empire where man is looking for a niche, communi-

54. John Brown was the militant abolitionist whose raid on the federal arsenal at Harpers Ferry, Virginia, in 1859, made him a martyr to the antislavery cause. Tried for murder, encouraging slave insurrection, and treason, he was convicted and hanged. Victor Hugo, one of the great influences on Dadié's thinking and writing, wrote a poem about him.

55. Dadié seems to conceive of this milk virus as prejudice based on color, a preference for white.

cation channels are ever-busy waterways for people and their products, all bearing on their back the label U.S.A. To take a break, these hustlers flee their extravagant cities for the old country, whose streets are sometimes crooked but where you can still sometimes find someone busy making nails in the corner of an alley; American nails die on the job and lie anonymously on the scrap heap. One glance at the perfect upkeep of airports reveals the passion here for travel: it's fair to say that many American citizens spend the greater part of their life between two airports. What can spouses do when men act like carrier pigeons? They spend most of their time on the telephone. What a pretty sight, this song-and-dance routine of long-distance communication. I look to the left; I look to the right; then I raise my eyes and burst out laughing. Parisians, notoriously malicious, would say they didn't know which foot to stand on.

I really have nothing against men, but I'd like them all to have double, triple, even quadruple chins, beautiful body ornaments that would raise them above the ordinary so you could see them emerging from their pipe smoke. For women, seemingly vestals in charge of who knows what new flame of a jealous god, I'd like to see something aristocratic, perhaps a fine, delicate mustache. After all, haven't these women also contributed to making America what she is? Isn't it their opinion that if you can put your feet up on a bed, it would be illogical not to be able to put them on a chair? Aren't they the ones who arrange mannequins in store windows and teach shoppers to stretch out their feet artfully in an easy chair? It was about time to rehabilitate feet: for thousands of years people had a tendency to scorn them and put them down, yet what would we do without our feet? It took America to give them a resting place, the footstool, and rightly so. Even though there are people who consider their feet worthless, the American foot is an important measure, one deserving a certain amount of respect. Without a footstool, where could we put it? To relax is to allow the foot to get some air, to breathe easily, to plunge into the ocean of surrounding air.

There are people who almost never know how and where to behave, but Americans do. Unencumbered by the useless weight of old customs, they can break everything and put it all back together in record time. Do they need a sponsor when they tend to become one for other nations?

*

* *

Factories are so deeply buried that porcelain hasn't yet seen the light of day. That will never do. Aren't there still people who eat and drink up in the trees? While we wait to be able to afford this classy product, we eat from a box, use plastic spoons and forks, and wipe our mouths with paper napkins nicely arranged to give priority to the entrance to that human factory—the stomach. The use of paper is spreading in every society. America is democratizing her classes, mixing and shaking them up, thanks to her paper plates. In one fell swoop she suppresses envy and jealousy in her customers, who, however, were already suppressed by the use of credit. Man has become a slave to money! American counts and millionaires seem closer to the people than those of other continents. And the country itself is a massive heart of gold which sometimes beats true.

Here as everywhere else in the world, people should stop all watches at mealtime: man seems to be the only motor that never stops running. Detaching the foot from its battery, the ground, and putting it on a chair removes the starter of the human motor. America is revolutionizing our habits by little discoveries that we're adopting just because they're new and sensational.

Soon we'll all be eating and drinking from paper plates to save time and effort and allow factories to keep running. Going back to paper renders homage to the simple life of so-called primitive peoples. And again it took America to bolster the ego of those peoples who—in order to seem civilized—eagerly fall in with the paper plate trend.

American power is magnetic and very bracing; it forces everyone to join the production line. A glass, a napkin, an apron, a napkin—do they not turn the machine's gear? In this land of commerce, the most harmless, insignificant gesture has precise repercussions.

*

* *

The capricious sun produces people in his likeness, sometimes exuberant, sometimes withdrawn, laughing one minute and blasé next; people who might be said to be suffering from stomach cramps that could erupt suddenly like a volcano. They don't even know how to say good-bye to a friend, walk along the sidewalk with him, shoot the breeze. It's time they enroll in our school to let their hearts open up freely. But how can they be open when they spend their whole life shut up in rooms? The weekend is not long enough to work a miracle. Stung by some insect, signaled by some interior beeper, have these walking transistors gotten some message? Right in the middle of a conversation, some will yell "bye," not even having the energy or time to make it "good-bye"! America saves effort, planning to create an energy bank. Yes, these people are the tightest, stingiest possible on earth. Six months here and I've never seen a "cent"[56] on the ground as I would at home. Fingers here must be magnets that never let a dime fall when taking change out or putting it back in—real magicians, playing with dollars trained always to return home, mission accomplished. Obviously, if every American were to drop a "cent" every day, America would quickly become a developing nation, just like an ordinary old newly freed colony: no one wants this—even those who labor in the new plantations, her factories.

How can people preoccupied with breaking their own production records afford to hold out their hand? To stop to extend a hand is to let the assembly line and luck go by, to disrupt action and actors, to break the rhythm of production. So Americans play the game of taking turns frightening each other, yelling "Hi! Hi!" every time they meet: the "Hello" is still too long and time-consuming. America is slowly leading the way back to the era of onomatopoeia, intending to demonstrate that man is really descended from apes and that the time is near when brother gorilla, cousin chimpanzee, aunt ape, and uncle zebra can welcome their long-lost relative—a malingerer on the path of evolutionary adventure.

"Hi! Hi!" A cry of pain that suggests someone has stepped on you. Having observed the quarrelsome gestures of American hands, it's understandable why a hand can't be extended to just anyone. Granted. But a hand shaking another hand, no matter how calloused, damp, soft, dirty, shaky, or steady, allows you to take the pulse of the speaker, feel the heartbeat, join bodies. How good it feels to shake and squeeze a friend's hand, to make troubles and worries, which others have hung there, fall off. To shake a hand is to welcome life. Human warmth, familial warmth—you hold all that when you grasp a hand.

Hi! American hands seem frozen. The whole world must drag them from their isolation, switch on their humanity, round off the sharp edges, offer a drink from the beaker of affection so that finally, no longer fearful of every little germ, Americans might know how to

56. Dadié seems to play on the word *cent,* meaning $100 in French and only a penny in English.

extend a hand to others, get a feel for them with their whole heart, a fine heart that many would like to bury in a coffin of gold.

Like a polar bird taking flight, they call out to you from their perch, "Hello." Just what kind of a human ambience can this country have when people don't even have time to look at each other, to care about each other or empathize? when doors remain closed to conserve their precious ration of air? when because no one wants to be bothered, there are butlers acting as jailers at every entrance? Have people gathered together only to be better separated into cells? The reason America is extending its borders is probably to improve such a climate.

A lack of both time and touch and myriad worries sometimes diminish the fullness of an otherwise winning smile. Its circles don't ring the face or round out the cheeks enough; they don't project enough fire in the eyes. This wan smile looks superficial, as if it comes from a wounded heart, a heart disillusioned, enslaved, trapped under thousands of layers of contradictory behavior. Might it be coming from a heart still in search of itself amidst a forest of buildings and machines? Of some not-yet-completed factory? It it synthetic? What a wonderfully dazzling smile America would have if she insisted on showing her gold teeth! A taste for the heady wines of Paris and Rome should also be adopted so that raised glasses would clink and send off sparks to warm their hands and make them stretch out and open up, unleash their hearts from coffee grounds and tea strings, and every residue of frustrated and unrequited love and unfulfilled dreams.

Having eyes and ears everywhere, America has understood the chink in her armor: how to reconcile the requirements of her way of life with those of other peoples? She hopes for simple solutions. The United Nations in New York provides the experimental field for offering her hand to other continents. Shaking the supple hand of a diplomat means shaking hands with four, ten, twenty million individuals of a state, all the while saving time, energy, and words. Moreover, it means leading the adversary to fight on a field chosen in advance, giving him the chance to appreciate the charms of American life.

Within the scope of the eternal mission of my country, if I were a Parisian billionaire, I'd assign myself the role of beckoning all Americans so that they might finally be able to shake hands among themselves and with others—an openly cordial handshake accompanied by a warm embrace.

*

* *

One of the questions that Americans have on the tip of their tongue, like a quid of tobacco, is: Are you married? to how many wives? Answer that you've only one and you disappoint them. They would like you to explain how you can have more than one wife and not crack. Their own wives are such weights, such burdens on their weak backs, that Americans no longer know which way to turn. I don't believe they're strong enough to support three or four women with character; women who are so headstrong, determined, and complete, for there's nothing sharper, more dynamic or irrevocable than the "no" of an American woman. It's a veritable sword she plunges into your heart as she smiles, studying your reactions. Here, they forget that a woman is trailing fifty sparkling stars behind her, to marry an American woman is to marry fifty-one stars. African women are content to play the woman trained to cushion shocks. How can I tell them all this? Best to wait until Americans become blacks—but who wants to be a black, one of those whose kids grow up in the shadow of factory smoke? in a group of huts haunted day and night by hungry fires? one of those stubborn men, who, despite so much misery, tells you "you must be born again"; a breed rooted in the soil, clutching life, refusing to die or disappear, wanting to be reborn, to live again, as if for unfinished business? Blacks are there like buoys oscillating in the white stream, at the will of the waves, like boundary markers along the highways on a journey of love. In this country of stones and pits, where they cultivate individualism and aggressiveness, where eyes reflect the color of gold, how can I explain that, where I live, women... Yes, it's true, we have to wait until they're mature, that is, black enough, before we tell them such important family secrets. In any case, they'd have to want to remain black, and for that to happen, night would have to fall on America, a night of one hundred years from which whites and blacks, mixed together in total darkness, would emerge into broad daylight to announce who's white and who's black! Indeed, America needs nighttime, a good, restful night of reflection for the enlightenment of hearts and minds.

This providential night—possibly heralding the birth of a new conception of human relations—might spread to other continents.

Even children, the epitome of innocence, wildly clap their hands when the president appears on television. What would be the attitude of the little ones if there were a black president, one to fulfill the desire of some Americans who want to leave the routine of the One Way, the old politics that keep America orbiting around Europe, a Europe that's not very happy to hear rumors of this new lioness near her shores?

*

* *

The leaves slowly turn the color of gold, then red; and one by one, two by two, are removed and blown away by the wind. A seasonal harvest. Children, who also sell empty bottles, love to watch the leaves turn yellow and fall off the trees where birds still come to sing and tell each other what they've seen in the world in the course of their wanderings. They call this season by an African name: Fall. Obviously, the rivalry around the estuaries of Senegalese rivers for the transportation of gold, gum, tusks, and ebony remains so vivid that only a Senegalese name would do for the ravages of time.

This slow agony of nature that lasts two months has given America an excessive gusto for life, an exacerbated combativeness in order to gain well-being, happiness, supremacy—whence come dishes packed with sugar, ice cream, and so many other goodies. Death is revealed at its best when, at the last minute before winter sets in, trees hoist delicate spring colors. Then, one by one, as if roasted, they take on the color black, ready to face the cold. This color of cloistered life, this mask life slips on to face a struggle, this shield which permits every victory here is taken as a sign of death. What do Americans know about symbolism? What do they learn from all those books? What do they observe in nature? or understand about everyday phenomena? Don't their priests put on black vestments to pray for eternal life? Doesn't the bride dress in white to mourn her lost freedom? And the groom strut around in black to crow about his victory? Of course, the real meaning of these colors remains a mystery. Obviously Americans are people who don't like the truth: truth would make the system on which they've built their existence crumble. They don't know that black allows life to be self-perpetuating. But it's true that the dead themselves turn pale, not black.

Leaves fall and put Americans to work. There they are, on little tractors, chasing leaves, but the wind keeps on shaking the branches, in a hurry to give them some sense of life after having stripped them. Fancy this insolent wind condemning the masters of the world to the sordid task of raking dead leaves!

Nature thus prepares to put on her annual shroud just as we cover our dead with white. White represents the rest that comes when life takes refuge under the color black. Is it really surprising that rhythm is essentially black? Black people boil with life, hang on to it, explode with vitality—distill it. That's why Harlem makes America live, makes her live a life that visibly sings and dances when blacks get out their drums. And this profound, fundamental ability to carry people away by the voice and the magic of the tam-tam makes American blacks African...

The slow death of nature incites Americans to return to their sources, to make a pilgrimage to the universities where they acquired the knowledge that made them big shots—first ladies, corporate directors, movers and shakers in world affairs, the greatest dancers, best physicists and actors in the world—and so America no longer has borders, having deliberately placed herself at the center of the universe.

This pilgrimage is a major event both for those who come back and for their hosts. Every night for weeks, students put away notebooks and books in order to make mascots and animals: their imagination is sorely tested. Various fraternities and dorms compete creatively. Students work until all hours to the sound of the twist blaring full force from loudspeakers that keep them awake and keep things humming. America without the twist would be a very sad nation indeed! The celebration, a kind of carnival, is like New Year's, except that American mascots, American animals, cats, and crows have strange proportions. Over the distance of many years, the celebration came to be known as Homecoming. Americans must have taken it from blacks when they were performing for masters who didn't always understand their language.

Homecoming is a prelude to the greatest national holiday, the holiday of thanks, Thanksgiving Day, an opportunity and an excuse for travel. That day restaurants stay open until dawn to serve the last hungry pilgrim.

Surrendering to winter, streets become silent; people safe at their home fireside become contemplative and relive the long journey since November 11, 1620, when the Mayflower brought the first pilgrims—fifty men, thirty women, thirty-four children; since the creation of the first newspaper in 1704, the *Boston Newsletter;* since the Declaration of Independence, July 4, 1776. It's basically a day to eat turkey, the big bird, to commemorate the alliance with the Redskins, who certainly showed their disloyal colors after all those love feasts. Holiday of meditation, of getting one's bearings with oneself, one's family, country, world, and with God. America's strength lies in her belief in a Supreme Being, who is thanked before meals and before drawing a sword. The American sword is the sword of the prophet, who no longer wants to waste time preaching in the urban desert. Thanksgiving ushers in Noel, Christmas Day, which lazy people write as X-mas. Ah! What would America be without machines? What will she become when her machines tire out? For now, Americans gloat over them as they watch them turn, but who knows what will happen tomorrow? Some of those machines could be stubborn; what a sight if America one day had no more energy to bully her machines? People don't dare think about that; in fact, for them it's an impossibility. They maintain that machines have so much civic spirit that they'd never try to paralyze the status quo, insured as it is against all risk. Machines can't go on strike! Americans are so confident of this that their prayers become passionate, so passionate that God, doubtless exasperated, revived for their benefit an old miracle.

One morning in December, at daybreak, the wind blew around first in one direction, then the other, a fine white dust falling from the sky—manna! The skeptical Americans stayed home to watch the manna pile on roofs, cars, and trees. Had they lost their taste for celestial things? Certainly giving manna to a whole town scarcely suffices to answer the personal prayer spoken from the bottom of the heart. Therefore, they refused to thank God, who, without worrying about them, kept on making His manna rain down.

Having made a pact with the serpent, the devil, this extraordinary man has the audacity to grow and eat apples, to drink apple juice, without having God raise a finger and set battalions of exterminating angels on his tail: this man believes he's worthy of respect especially when it concerns an event as important as making manna fall. He should have been warned. His radios should have announced the miracle days ahead to emphasize the fact that the Vaticanlike dome on the presidential palace signifies more than simple imitation. He believes that God changed continents for him. That God left the corridor mentality and serpentine ways of walled cities for open cities, candid American cities. America isn't a country to give the keys to the city to a visiting friend, for the simple reason that the pampas of cities have no ramparts. She hasn't fortified one city, but a whole nation—and the key to the state of fifty stars mustn't be given in homage to just anyone. If she ever gave away the keys to one of her large cities, they would only be false. Everyone knows this so well that her partners sometimes doubt American sincerity. False keys? Old customs found in American suitcases, just as old sorcerers leave their evil powers behind in their rags, as an inheritance. Since Europe no longer recognizes her own customs because the keys from Pacific factories have become bigger and heavier, isn't that the most obvious sign of progress? In this country, where the age of actresses, their marital status, even when they crossed the Cape of Good Hope are broadcast; where everyone in offices and meetings wears name tags; where White House is also the name of a powerful and old business firm—who can be accused of duplicity? What game can be hidden when four or five revolutionary cities of Paris are carried in her bosom? If tomorrow the French needed another model of their capital, they could find a copy either in Texas or in Arkansas. Vincennes awaits them in Kentucky, ready to be delivered as spare parts. They've become prefabricated cities, thus, reviewed, corrected, and improved. With their own peculiar habits, that hotels treat with a certain distance, American tourists can go there for spring vacations without feeling disoriented. After all, isn't this home? "Come again," he'll say to the Parisian the day of his return to the land of Liberty. Isn't it a basic contradiction to have a border when you're trying to unite states and people? Drawing people together—ossified by the practices of millennia—sometimes means shifting boundaries or being themselves displaced. As soon as he can stand up, an American thinks about a car and an RV: he needs the horizon, bird songs, butterfly flights to recharge himself. He's a great but misunderstood poet lambasted for attaching too much value to the dollar and insisting it increase threefold. Americans know that poor poets, who're never either valued or taken seriously, are treated like gypsies, even if the pearls they drop are purer than gold or diamonds. They understand the world they live in and the values men respect: that's why they give gold and the dollar priority so everyone can be aware of the inestimable value of man.

Poet, businessman, soldier, and boss! The American galley houses dark holds hidden by luminous masts. Nevertheless this country is alive because she wants to be told what's not working in her myriad gears. This is one of the basic strengths of this huge state that sleeps with one eye open on the world.

Cannibalism was born because men who'd been naked for so long began to appreciate here a calf or a thigh, there a cheek or a neck. To protect the human species it was urgent to give him clothes and shoes. Now we have too much luxury in some places, in others too much poverty, and this leads people to despise each other. People have learned to judge each other by the clothes they wear, superficial judgments by people in a hurry to end a discussion. To close the gap, American factories produce night and day with no letup, insisting that men finally rise above the tinsel. Gigantic tasks to which all peoples must buckle down in order for the human ship to regain its balance. America invites all nations to this noble task, convinced, nevertheless, that if man didn't suffer, he couldn't possibly get to heaven. A god who wants to be martyred through man, who can be assassinated for an ounce of gold or some rags! Others remain skeptical. Experience has taught that to make friends with the great is always to end up in their belly. Hasn't America annexed the outstanding leaders—Napoleon, Hannibal, Bismark? Hasn't she made them her mentors and confined them to her borders so that their example won't contaminate new conquerors? This is the response of the Boss, who intends to place all war under the patronage of Liberty. Henceforth, war becomes civilized. It loses its plundering nature and leaves the corner of the woods for public spaces, becoming what men judge to be a necessary evil in their evolution. Loyal guardian of the Great Statue, powerful fetish of the empire, America won't undertake anything without having placed herself in her shadow, which lends depth, weight, and scale to her actions. Loving neither ambiguity nor obscurity, this country takes a foreigner in hand as soon as he crosses the border in order to enlighten him by showing her many illustrious leaders, accomplishments, and victories. Doesn't she want to be the voluntary guinea pig for the strange life of tomorrow—a mechanized existence where enormous, taciturn, and exhausted crowds line up for the bus, concerts, the plane, love, etc.? By her example, America illustrates the future community. But who can understand her way of talking? Stoically tied down to an uncongenial occupation, deafened by a noise and music that's taken her offtrack, America is tinkering with her system to find an out. In vain! The machine is encircling her on all sides, molding her people to a model soon to be patented in order that America can keep her basic character, especially after the whole world has adopted her tricks and trends. Standing in a line leading to decadence and death like every nation and empire, America clings to the world to avoid sinking under her gold and machines and suffocating under the weight of her dollars. How will she die? Though no one dares say it, everyone thinks the prodigy lacks a certain amount of experience that could hold her back from the brink of extremism...

The snow falls. Mouth and ears steaming, people lower their head to face it. They charge the cold weather like the bull charging the toreador—straight ahead.

Covered with a white veil, the sun has lost its warmth. Scarcely has it appeared at the edge of the American border when it immediately begins its descent. Is it afraid of these men who walk showing their teeth, ready to bite who knows whom? Yes, Americans aren't really peaceful people. How can friends be attracted when menacing teeth are shown for no legitimate reason? And so all the passers-by are crying as if an imminent calamity were going to befall the country. Women blow their nose every minute, the tapering tips reddening. At this time of the year, the blessed cold prayed for diligently by drinking cold drinks, by repeatedly eating cold meals, has now set their feet on fire.[57] The cold has disastrous results, making them reveal their true selves—ambitious men in a hurry.

*
* *

How beautiful is this white rug spread over the land, the trees, and houses! How pleasant to admire the fine powder tossed by the wind and placed on the edge of windows, branches—everywhere! Taking refuge inside homes, heat announces its presence from chimneys. The earth is resting so that man, that beast of burden, won't kill himself, for he is capable of never feeling fatigue enter and drag him down since he's intent on fattening his bank account. Are we not on a continent where work kills men instead of allowing them to live? To eliminate sloth, hasn't America enslaved men to machines and money and, by indoctrination, allowed them to see themselves as a by-product of gold—the exact opposite of our conception of the relationship between man and money. Only wealth counts: age, experience, and wisdom no longer have cachet. And yet they were here before money made its appearance. They're so precious now that no thief has ever been able to steal them and no one has ever been able to bequeath them. A society that honors those other values, the ones that can never be devalued by a simple stock market transaction—is it uncivilized?

Shut off by the nature of things, American farmers, champing at the bit, are making plans for the new year. They're waiting for spring to take on her brilliant colors again. On this side of the ocean, you've got to work hard to endure the rigors of winter. Hasn't nature given us three months' respite? Have we forgotten? Fortunately it's different in our country. The Creator spared us the rigors of cold and gave us a different work rhythm. We can understand the attitude of fortune hunters in certain parts of the world. Living in constant fear of a winter

57. The expression in French is *mettre le feu aux trousses,* translated to convey the image of heat.

that never came, they watched, undisturbed, as battalions of men made to serve them vanished.

Snow as far as the eye can see—a few people, a few birds, a cadaver of a sun, skeletons of trees, a thin wisp of smoke coming from a chimney—all emphasize that Life outranks Death. Americans, however, observe their main holiday in spring, when the sap rises in every living thing.

Women are thrilled to see men finally working. Considering what they do, wives are right to go to work in offices in order to prevent them from making mistakes. These men love to spread salt on the snow, hoping to see it grow and produce. Their ancestors did it, and so do they. Does the god of snow have a weakness for salt? However, these men are so impatient that, several minutes later, seeing no salt rising, they arm themselves with shovels to clear the snow and salt, dumping them in the same waste bin. Every bit equal to these remarkable workers, the women quicken the pace, pouting. Men pretend not to notice. For once they're given the chance to work outside, in the street in front of witnesses, and they're not about to miss it without marking the occasion. It's hardly their fault if they can do nothing with their hands; they're accustomed to supervising and watching others work. This has given them a bizarre mentality. The American who asks you a question will immediately think of the answer he'd have given rather than yours. It's what he thinks that matters. Not surprisingly his curiosity in certain areas is very limited. What advice can a boss of international status need, watching over a multitude of nations from his eagle's nest?

* * *

X-mas! a popular holiday, demonstrating to all the exuberance of American faith—a thirst for redemption, a burning desire to re-create Eden! Lampposts are decorated with lights, horses, and illuminated angels; open-air mangers spring up in front of service stations, department stores, and on the roofs of drug stores. Boutiques are festive, and everyone boasts a smile. Christ is coming again, to save them. Prices rise like an arrow to meet the miraculous star. American merchants insist on rehabilitating brother Judas, who failed to sell Jesus at a proper price. Foolish and shortsighted, Iscariot was so simpleminded that he didn't discover until later what a fortune he could've made with his

Jesus! Imagine hanging yourself for thirty denarii when money now sanctified by holy institutions produces holy dividends! Poor Judas; throughout the centuries he's been repeatedly burned by the people in their Passion plays.

Out in the cold, Jesus becomes a service station owner, maybe even pumping gas, while angels up on the roof sound the trumpet to attract clients. It's clear that America was as yet undiscovered in Judas's time—a heaven-sent gift because Jesus certainly would have chosen this business paradise, this new temple, in order to come shake up the stock market. Here, a heightened sense of opportunity is emphasized. You must earn accolades and salaries. Jesus and his large following of angels, shepherds, magi, and animals are asked to prove what they can do and to submit references which will make them acceptable. Right off it's recommended that He no longer choose the night to be born: it would be useless to have daylight or sunlight if a god, paradoxically, were only born at night. Americans, who separate night and day, black and white, into watertight compartments, take a dim view of such ambiguity. Surely midnight is a happy hour, the marriage of sunset and dawn; both display the same colors as if to emphasize the continuity of time, the futility of counting years—nonetheless, it's nighttime. If Christ's doctrine still hasn't conquered the darkness after thousands of years, it's because He was born at a time when people were sleeping. The angels' songs resulted in a dreamlike state from which men seem not yet to have awakened. Let Him be born then, the good Jesus, just a little before the final whistle but not when workers are lining up for the bus or running to catch a taxi on a rainy day. Above all "don't be late." Isn't He the only one who can solve the great problem of racism which the whole world accuses America of deliberately provoking? Today's people have nothing against their black brothers, but they do hold a grudge against their ancestors for lacking the courage to integrate into the community the results of their heroic deeds. What else did the white man have to do during the three winter months but to mate—a funny character, cock, goose, peacock, and cuckoo all rolled into one. Blacks would have too much to say if they could speak. How many families would blush at their revelations, and how many whites would become black from one moment to the next! Americans only give them the floor after they've passed a thousand tests, after they're sure blacks have crossed the line of morality and changed color. A death in the camp of white brothers, a prisoner of honor, a white flag.

X-mas. Christ will come again. What a catastrophe if a black were the first to talk to Him. It's important to stay alert. As they prepare to welcome Jesus, everyone lights up their homes and places bouquets of flowers on doors. Jesus loves colors, all colors, especially in a bouquet; the bouquet of human colors that He had originally created remains close to his heart. Americans light up their homes and fill them with flowers, but they close their hearts to colors and only half-open the door. Jesus is coming! Where will He stay? Will He prefer motels, YMCAs, the luxurious Sheraton chain? The manger? The latter no longer exists. To preserve the steers, cows, and sheep, they've canned them and shelved them in grocery stores. Couldn't they sell Jesus and spare those who were with Him when he was born? Let Him come at last, this Jesus, to bring peace to the races, for His rainbow has never tried to put down roots on earth.

The fate of animals has been settled: they're good for belly and bank. Jesus should refrain from asking about his old friends, those creatures who, after thousands of years of collaboration with men, have neither learned to walk upright nor speak, even less to behave like men. Several of them ruminate just like men, but is that enough proof to consider them evolved? Oh, what a mover and shaker this Jesus is! On with His arrival then and be done with it!

The only tree to keep its leaves in this period of deadly cold is the fir, which has become the symbol of vegetable vitality, of life—the quintessential Christian tree that remains alert for the second coming. Everyone associates the fir with New Year's ceremonies. The respect granted it is so great that people have become troubled and confused. In this country no one could imagine Christmas without one—it's a fetish, a good luck charm that merchants sell for high prices. There it stands, adorned and lighted, to assist and participate in the communal joy, to infuse a bit of its life into everyone. Children pray to it, important people confide in it—all family life during Christmas holidays goes on under its branches. Look at these animists, pretending to be freed of all ties to ghosts and spirits. Their fear of ghosts is so great that they don't make real tombs for the dead: they obviously bury them standing, place stone slabs on their heads to prevent them from coming back to haggle over hamburgers and milk. A very curious people, apparently searching for the right way, yet weighed down at the neck by the heavy chains of the One Way. All these—the bright streets, the neon-lighted stores, the glimmering, multicolored villas, the angels on the roof, the manger at the foot of the gas pumps—all share only one goal and one mission: to show the American way to Jesus on His next trip. Here in America at least, even though His ideas have not evolved, He won't be made to carry a cross. A country in the forefront of progress wouldn't copy the vulgar Palestinian Jews. An electric chair is ready, and bets are on that, after this fling, He will no longer ever have any desire to come back to earth to upset the grievously painful ascent of man. The Jews missed him; the Americans won't. You don't crucify a god, you cremate him: you neither throw divine ashes to the wind nor on the water... but after all, why be anxious? Haven't some people already solved the problem? Could all those lights be merely traps? If so, this explains why Jesus won't stop in America. He is waiting for men to form the human bouquet that He absolutely insists on; for blacks to have a voice in order to sing His praises just like whites; for the two to blend their voices so that songs in churches will stop being about Hell for some and about joy for others—for unison. He's waiting for man to finally shed his golden cocoon and rise above the colors that are tearing him apart. Americans remain watchful, fearful that another nation will be preferred, so they light up everything, including monuments to the dead, where gigantic crosses shine. In a vault, a golden donkey awaits the heavenly cavalier, who's no longer going to have to multiply loaves, since Americans have decided to go one better. A thousand "jets" loaded with food, and there you have it—a miracle accomplished! Americans await the fateful day and, for Christmas, drink something special, eggnog, made with eggs, milk, sugar, cream, vanilla, rum, and whiskey. They offer God their best, just as we offer Him fresh eggs, flour, and our first yams through the intercession of our close neighbors, the spirits. This similarity in customs might lead us to believe that Americans are blacks, having continuously left Africa from time immemorial. No matter how much it hurts to admit it, where else but from blacks could Americans have gotten the habit of giving a drink to strangers? Go into any restaurant and you'll be given a glass of water even before the menu. Where did they get this excellent practice of "resting the heart" if not from Africa?

Imagine how many temples, churches, and other religious buildings, how many statues and altars would go up in flames in all the Southern states (not all are American or Boer) if people knew that Jesus had black blood in His veins, that is, red, not white, blood! Oh yes—Jesus was a black with red blood in His veins—a disconcerting fact for those who insist on tracking down their brothers over such a silly matter as color. If, by chance, they also had red blood, there'd be proof that they, too, were blacks; and the racial struggle would become nothing more than ridiculous fratricide.

The gigantic Statue of Liberty must have been a gift from the friends of blacks to America, a land where all the blacks of the world, fleeing the hell of their own countries, came to seek refuge. Paris had no choice but to give this land of superlatives a colossal Liberty that would hold its own against skyscrapers and bring them to terms. Who wouldn't have been embarrassed, amazed, and overwhelmed by such excessive freedom? America, not yet fully recovered from her astonishment, is still searching for its way in the shadow of Liberty.

*
* *

For a long time now, the moon's been in the sky, inviting people to dance, but no one pays any attention. But to give off free light is setting a pernicious example; so Americans have declared war on the moon and hatched a bold scheme to bring it back to earth to repair the harm it's done to the national economy. They're spending sums like crazy in this endeavor and, at the same time, letting certain of their compatriots, those who aren't flashy enough to attract attention, die of poverty. Naturally, lunar light, which eclipses the light of the fifty stars, comes across as a provocation, an affront, so even those dying of hunger joyously accept dying so that the moon can finally be brought to reason, made to toe the American line.

From time to time, the sun and the moon cross paths, as an example to all people imprisoned in their color. But they barely lift their nose to see what's happening in the sky. The American is a modest person, one who never observes what's happening above his head, especially in the heavens.

Isn't the Bible full of divine prophecies? But what can blacks, standing on distant shores among the Iroquois, still understand of this old style? A highway builder, the American always knows which exit to take to escape right under your nose. Think he's approaching? No, he's going another way. He's on another wavelength, participating in another conference, speaking another language. He approaches, then retreats. In another orbit, the American's become a planet whose evolutions must be carefully watched.

Most to be pitied in America are the artists—especially painters who don't know how to mix black and white into a harmonious whole and thus achieve the requisite charm for their works. Most are bald or very gray. If these painters were to achieve the wonderful miracle of blending black and white, who'd dare buy a painting dealing with revolution? American blacks would be the first in line to put it in restaurant windows, along streets—like an agenda! But no one would sell it to him, knowing his subversive ideas on black-white relations. Women would like to challenge this position. Why fear blacks when they've had the audacity to trample the Serpent himself? Their men are very frightened, however, and beg them not to tempt these diabolical men whose primitive mold still holds firm and continues to reveal itself in all sorts of ways, even after centuries of contact with the world's masters: the fire in their eye, the sun in their voice, their loose way of walking, their spontaneous relationships and frenetic passion for music and dance. Nonetheless, the American varnish peels off many marginal blacks: they sing and dance "you are my sunshine" and point to another continent in their background. It's sad to see this ardent fire burn in the hearts of millions who live here like outcasts, shipwrecked on a reef, hopelessly signaling to all passing boats loaded with human rights. Yet for the glory of their country, they continue to give their brawn and their dreams: they're one of the largest turbines making America run.

In Washington, D.C., the capital, where political alliances are made and unmade, blacks are among those who offer flowers for all occasions from romance to rupture. Could their flowers be powerful enough to heal wounds and bring peace to hearts? Standing at the bedstead of their America, whom they'd like to see as a generous, smiling fairy godmother, blacks watch over everyone in complexes and hotels. They're even part of the White House guard. These jacks-in-the-box, having lost their aggressive mechanism, no longer frighten, so their stock's gone up in American hearts. America assimilates its colors. After the United States come the United Colors, melted down in the hearts and minds of citizens to give true stability to the nation and make her the authentic country of Liberty, champion of fraternity. No one, then, among all those who skillfully massacre their blacks without dirtying their hands, can any longer throw the first stone at America. It's been a very difficult birth, and one that should be speeded up by appropriate dances. After the leaps of rock 'n' roll, America, contorted by shooting birth pains, writhes to the twist, making, so it seems, an effort to exit from a cocoon, a matrix, to break the ties which bind her.

This slow, painful birth, which will free the nation from all the iron fists holding it captive, makes all the patriotic beds of Washington, D.C., insomniacs.

However, this American attempt to overcome the steel grip and the technological rigor paralyzing her, and the sleepless nights the president spends trying to save, preserve, and augment the heritage—all that makes Washington's jaded, grumbling, and grousing beds light-headed with joy. A treaty that doesn't end up at their feet isn't binding, and the president knows it.

The effort unleashed by America to brake the boasting of some of the newly rich, whose endless appetites suggest that the dollar is the weightiest money to carry, the most demanding in the world, the most diabolical of the moment, the classiest of the era, inspires delirious enthusiasm in Washington's musical chairs.

The longer diplomats and politicians remain calm and silent, scornful and mute, the longer capital beds remain nervous, sensitive, exuberant, and talkative.

Whether Democrat or Republican, these extremely ticklish "marine" beds, trained for any landing, yell war "cries" as soon as a foreigner penetrates their domain. They mark him by his scent and his movements.

How about staying calm or I'll rouse the whole neighborhood.
American legs don't work that way...
Oh, no! here no one snores and no one sleeps with both ears closed.
Go on, get up, it's my turn to rest!

Full of every American enthusiasm, every street and factory sound, and steeped in bold dreams, these beds help every museum curator, every librarian, every tourist executive to grind out the important dates and facts of the country's history.

And they are diabolically adept at mixing cards and dealing them to people who've never seen each other. Thus it was that one day I had, as a neighbor, a smiling Viennese lady here to visit the New Eden. Thanks to the Parisian language, we were able to communicate and talk about the great factory that is America. Well, the night of the meeting, my bed made such a din that the next day the neighbor's face wore such an inscrutable expression that her eyes were barely visible. To her I was a poor sleeper. How could she know that I was the occupant of a bed whose wood works and sings for encouragement?

Beds:
Diplomats—polite and discreet
Orators—the spitting image of their master, never leaving the microphone

Cowboys and Jazz—hideaway or not, twin or not, iron or wood...
  antique or modern
Whatever their size, weight, number of feet, color, shape, degree of
  sensitivity

  aggressiveness
  rebelliousness

Whatever their suppleness, tribal mark, appearance, sleep quality,
  references

  service—soldiers or not
  reserve or not
  retired or not

Friends of every color and opinion...[58]

Beware the beds of Washington, D.C. They're all answerable to the FBI and ready to sacrifice themselves as a last resort, and to their last gasp, for the greatness of their country.

They too are the United States of America, and they want everyone to know it.

To give heart and soul to factory products, to compel them to fill their role scrupulously, what better way to accomplish such a beautiful feat than the One Way?

No wonder the whole world is signing up for America's school.

New York, March 18, 1963.

58. I turned this paragraph into a free poem in order to illustrate the exuberance of Dadié's language, reaching as it does a crescendo in the last pages.

BERNARD BINLIN DADIÉ, born in 1916 in Assinie (Ivory Coast), is one of Africa's major writers. A co-founder, with Alioune Diop, of Présence Africaine, he has also been a prominent political figure, both before his country's independence and in the Ministries of Education and Information. He was Minister of Culture from 1977 until his retirement from public life a few years ago.

JO PATTERSON is an instructor in French and English at Northwest Community College in Terrace, B.C. A native of North Carolina, she has lived in Canada since 1980. The subject of her Ph.D. dissertation was Bernard Dadié.